Say Please,
Little Bear

This edition published by Parragon in 2012

Parragon
Queen Street House
4 Queen Street
Bath BA1 1HE, UK
www.parragon.com

ISBN 978-1-4454-8362-7

Printed in China

Say Please, Little Bear

Story by Peter Bently

Illustrations by Robert McPhillips

PaRragon

Bath • New York • Singapore • Hong Kong • Cologne • Delhi
Melbourne • Amsterdam • Johannesburg • Auckland • Shenzhen

Daddy Bear and Little Bear were on their
way to playgroup.
But Little Bear kept wandering off.

"Keep hold of my
hand, Little Bear!"
said Daddy Bear.

"Go gently, Little Bear!"
said Daddy Bear at playgroup.

But Little Bear didn't listen.

"Little Bear, it isn't nice to snatch!"

"It's better when
we share, Little Bear,"
said Daddy Bear.

Later, Daddy Bear took Little Bear to
Little Bunny's birthday party.
They went shopping on the way.
"Please hold my hand, Little Bear!"
said Daddy Bear wearily.

Then something in the shop window
gave Daddy Bear an idea.
"Look, Little Bear," he said.
"Mouse wants to speak to us!"

TOY SHOP

"Mouse wants to come to the party too, Little Bear," said Daddy Bear. "But he hates to be late!"

They reached Little Bunny's party on time.
Mouse whispered in Daddy Bear's ear.

"Mouse says, excuse me, please,"
said Daddy Bear.

Little Bear ran to play on the train.
Mouse whispered in Daddy Bear's ear again.
"Mouse says,
can she have
a ride on the
train, please?"

Little Bear snatched the popcorn from his friends.
Mouse whispered in Daddy Bear's ear once again.
"Mouse says, would *you* like some popcorn,
Bunny and Mole?"

When it was
time to go,
Little Bear
stood silently
on the doorstep.
"Mouse says,
thank you for
having me,"
said Daddy Bear.

Little Bear looked at Mouse. Then he looked at Daddy Bear. Then he looked at Little Bunny's mummy and said, "And thank you for having me."

"Oh, thank you for coming, Little Bear,"
smiled Little Bunny's mummy.

"You and Mouse can
come and play any time."

"Mouse likes the way
you said thank you,"
said Daddy Bear.

"And so do I."

anatomy of
STRENGTH &
CONDITIONING

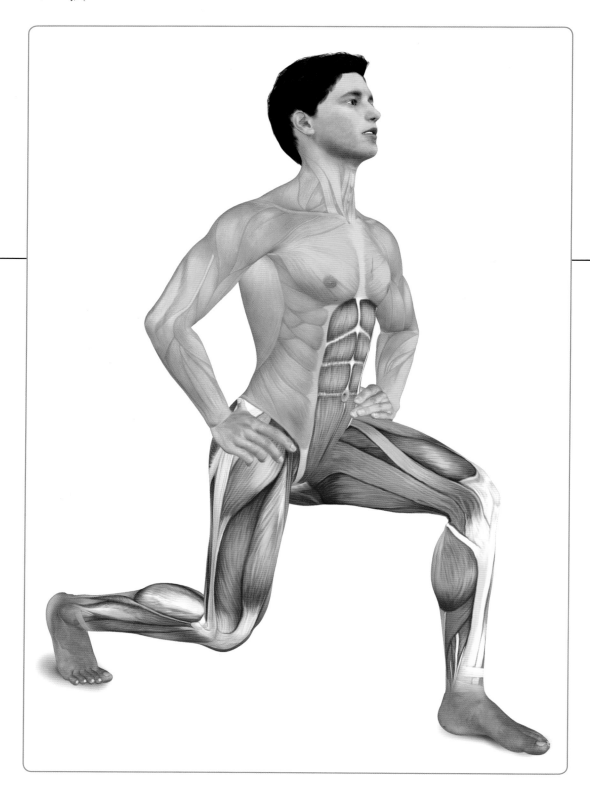

anatomy of
STRENGTH &
CONDITIONING

Hollis Lance Liebman

B L O O M S B U R Y

LONDON · NEW DELHI · NEW YORK · SYDNEY

Published by Bloomsbury Publishing Plc
50 Bedford Square
London WC1B 3DP
www.bloomsbury.com

First edition 2013

Copyright © 2013 Moseley Road Inc.

ISBN 978 1 4081 8999 3

A CIP catalogue record for this book is available from the British Library.

Moseley Road Inc.
President: Sean Moore
General Manager: Karen Prince
Art Director: Tina Vaughan
Production Director: Adam Moore

Editors: David & Sylvia Tombesi-Walton
Designer: Simon Murrell

Photographer: Fine Arts Photography
Models: Miguel Carrera, Tara DiLuca

This book is produced using paper that is made from wood grown in managed, sustainable forests. It is natural, renewable and recyclable. The logging and manufacturing processes conform to the environmental regulations of the country of origin.

Printed and bound in China by Oceanic Graphic Printing (OGP)

10 9 8 7 6 5 4 3 2 1

CONTENTS

INTRODUCTION

The aim of strength and conditioning training is to enable you not only to handle a heavier load but also to carry that load in a better way. This is achieved by improving your aerobic capacity through the grouping together of various types of exercise. In plain speak, we are talking about enabling greater performance through increased strength, speed, capacity and accuracy. It is only through the continual application and eventual mastery of these four skill sets that an athlete can achieve his or her best.

INTRODUCTION

Strength training and conditioning, though different in definition and result, are reliant on one another and complement each other perfectly. A strong athlete may be able to lift an enormous load, but this is of limited use if he or she doesn't also have the conditioning and requisite lung capacity to go the distance in a chosen discipline. It also follows that an athlete with great stamina but lacking explosive power will not reach his or her full potential.

Generally speaking, a bigger muscle tends to be a stronger muscle; however, one need not be overly developed to showcase unparalleled strength. This is because the best, most rounded sporting performance depends on the application of four major elements: strength, speed, capacity and accuracy. Combining strength training with conditioning work allows an athlete to master these skill sets; he or she will not only be able to handle a heavier load but will also develop greater aerobic capacity.

WHAT IS STRENGTH TRAINING?

In its simplest terms, strength training can be defined as the act of moving a weight from point A via point B to point C. Although straightforward,

this pathway requires progressively more effort, forcing the muscle to work increasingly hard. Performance in strength training can be compared to that of a coiled spring – first, there is a slow winding or cranking of the muscle; and then a quick, explosive release. A very obvious example of this is the Barbell Power Clean and Jerk (see page 38), in which the barbell is lifted first off the floor and to the chest (the movement from A to B), then from the chest to an overhead position (the movement from B to C). A few repetitions of this type of muscular contraction will result in increased anaerobic output and muscular power.

Strength training usually calls for the assistance of a group of muscles to complete a multi-jointed movement. The squat, for example –

The Kettlebell Figure 8 helps build strength in your abdominal muscles.

perhaps the ultimate exercise for lower-body strength – is widely considered a thigh exercise; however, it also uses the glutes, hamstrings and core muscles to stabilise the body properly during motion and to 'fire' during execution. This synergistic combination of opposing body parts working together to complete a given movement is an important difference between strength training and conventional bodybuilding. In the latter, the tendency is to isolate and focus on one muscle, minimising help from neighbouring ancillary tissue in order to keep tension primarily on the target. A bodybuilder wishing to work the biceps, for example, would perform seated dumbbell curls, because the seated position ensures that assistance from the lower back is kept to a minimum.

Strength training also differs from bodybuilding because its focus is not on increasing muscle tissue and bulk, refining proportions or creating symmetry; it is not about how big your chest or arms are

or the compactness of your waist. The real goal of strength training is quite simply increased strength and muscular power.

Any type of strength-focused exercise results in the muscles being broken down through microscopic tears that occur during muscular overload. Bodybuilders often train to the point of absolute muscular failure (that is, the inability to complete a movement due to inadequate strength), because the effort of the muscle to repair itself contributes and leads to increased muscle mass. However, since the goal in strength training is increased power rather than bulk, it is not necessary to lift the maximum weight you can manage for the highest number of repetitions you can achieve. As a result, recuperation time is shortened, which means that you can train more often and see results more quickly. Nevertheless, you should avoid over-training or training to the point of excessive body fatigue and lethargy. Aim to incorporate strength training into your regime no more than three

The Medicine Ball Pike-Up is perfect for increasing strength and stability in your core.

9

or four days per week, focusing on correct form and execution rather than on marathon sessions. Throughout this book, the number of repetitions performed in strength exercises is high enough for you to test and improve upon your current strength levels, but low enough not to exert too much stress on your body.

WHAT IS CONDITIONING?

Conditioning, a type of training based on constant motion performed for ever-increasing amounts of time, is less about strength and more about fitness. This aerobic activity is usually executed at high speed.

Since the goal of conditioning is improved performance and an increased aerobic output and efficacy when completing a given movement, muscle tissue is not broken down.

This eliminates the need for the rest and repair that is required after anaerobic training.

This type of training often necessitates a high number of repetitions or is carried out in time increments. Its success is dependent on continual body movement, often of the full body, incorporating speed, balance, stability and accuracy. A person who is well conditioned is able to use his or her body at physically strenuous levels for prolonged periods of time. Combining conditioning with the explosive power gleaned from strength training makes for a very well-rounded individual, athletically speaking.

Whereas strength training is limited to a given and predictable routine, the possibilities in conditioning exercises are almost infinite. Elements such as speed, direction, impact and breathing pattern can all be altered during this

EQUIPMENT

The Anatomy of Strength and Conditioning programme requires various pieces of equipment, illustrated here.

Kettlebells
These spherical items, available in various weights, have a flat bottom and thick handle.

Rollers
Often fashioned out of polystyrene, these cylindrical tools help relieve tension and combat muscle waste.

Barbells and Dumbbells
Whether fixed-weight or adjustable, these are the building blocks of strength training.

type of workout to 'confuse' the body, forcing it to adapt in terms of performance.

PLANNING YOUR ROUTINE

In terms of training implementation, I recommend you start by rolling out any sore and restricted muscles (see pages 16–20). This will help 'open up' the muscle cells and loosen any tight tissue in preparation for the demanding work to follow.

Stretching (see pages 21–25) can and should be performed only once the muscles are warm in order to prevent the tearing that can occur as a result of forcing a muscle past its cold, or 'non-warm', threshold.

The strength portion of your workout is next, followed by conditioning exercises and concluding with stretching. This second period of stretching helps remove any toxins from pumped muscles and aids recuperation.

Your weekly routine should consist of three to four strength workouts and four conditioning workouts. The conditioning should follow on from or be mixed in with the strength work. It is essential to take at least one rest day per week, preferably two, to allow the muscles to heal and recuperate, therefore making them able to handle heavier loads and challenges in the weeks ahead. Unlike a traditional bodybuilding workout, which includes myriad angles and positions, this strength and conditioning programme focuses on ten or so movements that hit the muscle groups and their ancillary tissues to help make you as strong and well conditioned as possible.

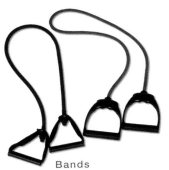

Bands
These are rubber resistance bands used in strength training.

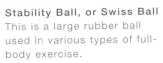

Jump Box
This is used in plyometric training.

Medicine Ball
This small, firm rubber ball is used in various full-body exercises.

Cone
In plyometric exercises, this is used as a target, a point of reference or an obstacle.

Stability Ball, or Swiss Ball
This is a large rubber ball used in various types of full-body exercise.

FULL-BODY ANATOMY

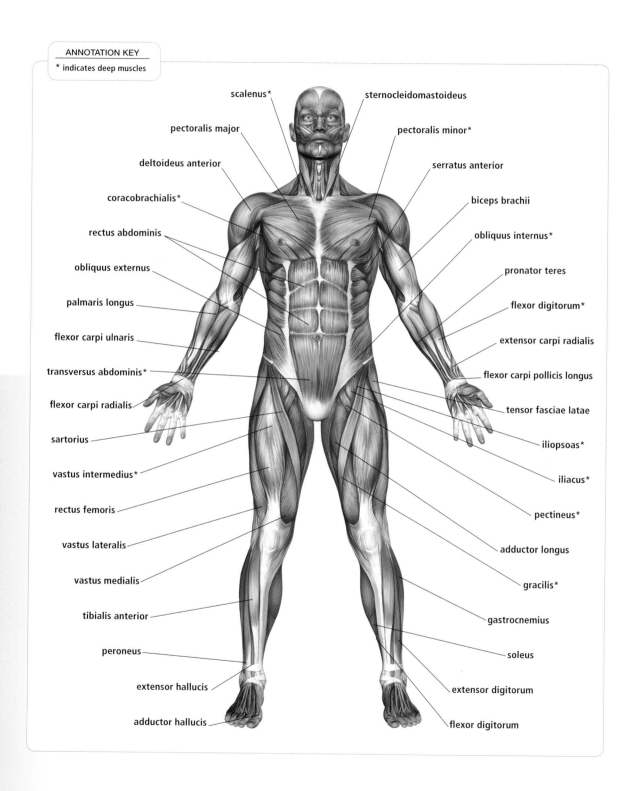

ANNOTATION KEY
* indicates deep muscles

scalenus*

sternocleidomastoideus

pectoralis major

pectoralis minor*

deltoideus anterior

serratus anterior

coracobrachialis*

biceps brachii

rectus abdominis

obliquus internus*

obliquus externus

pronator teres

palmaris longus

flexor digitorum*

flexor carpi ulnaris

extensor carpi radialis

transversus abdominis*

flexor carpi pollicis longus

flexor carpi radialis

tensor fasciae latae

sartorius

iliopsoas*

vastus intermedius*

iliacus*

rectus femoris

pectineus*

vastus lateralis

adductor longus

vastus medialis

gracilis*

tibialis anterior

gastrocnemius

peroneus

soleus

extensor hallucis

extensor digitorum

adductor hallucis

flexor digitorum

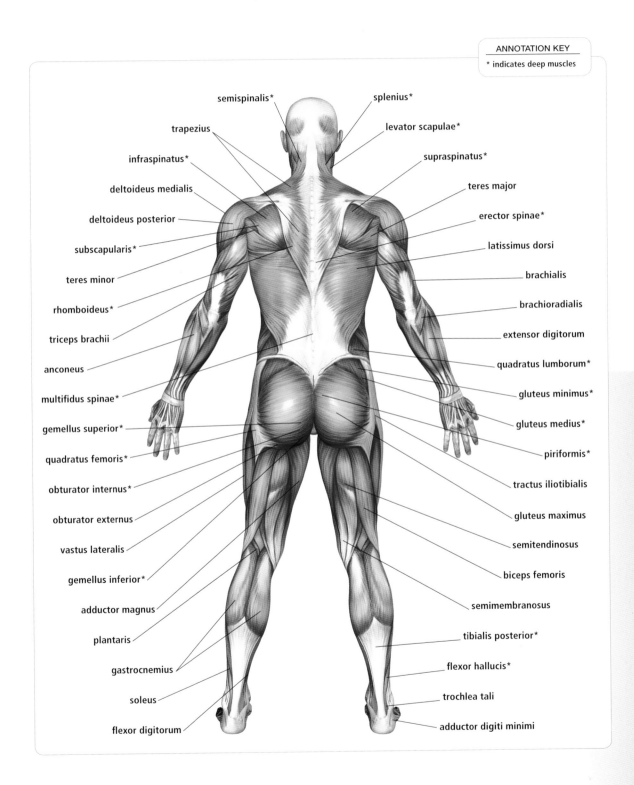

ANNOTATION KEY

* indicates deep muscles

semispinalis*

splenius*

trapezius

levator scapulae*

infraspinatus*

supraspinatus*

deltoideus medialis

teres major

deltoideus posterior

erector spinae*

subscapularis*

latissimus dorsi

teres minor

brachialis

rhomboideus*

brachioradialis

triceps brachii

extensor digitorum

anconeus

quadratus lumborum*

multifidus spinae*

gluteus minimus*

gemellus superior*

gluteus medius*

quadratus femoris*

piriformis*

obturator internus*

tractus iliotibialis

obturator externus

gluteus maximus

vastus lateralis

semitendinosus

gemellus inferior*

biceps femoris

adductor magnus

semimembranosus

plantaris

tibialis posterior*

gastrocnemius

flexor hallucis*

soleus

trochlea tali

flexor digitorum

adductor digiti minimi

13

WARM-UP
EXERCISES

When undertaking any sort of physical training, it is important to start by warming up your muscles, since this will make them more pliable and thus less susceptible to injury. Self-myofascial release (or rolling) therapy is an effective warm-up that involves the use of a foam roller to ease out any knots deep within the muscle tissue, improve flexibility and performance, and reduce the risk of injury.

Although not strictly part of a warm-up regime, stretching should be carried out both during and after training to keep your muscles strong and pliable. Stretching also increases blood supply to the joints, helps relieve pain and stress, boosts energy levels, and improves posture.

ROLLING: HAMSTRINGS

❶ Begin in a seated position, with a foam roller placed underneath your upper legs, and your hands either to the side or behind you for support. Bend your left leg and shift your weight on to the right leg.

BEST FOR
- biceps femoris
- semitendinosus
- semimembranosus

❷ Keeping your right foot off the floor, begin rolling over the belly of the muscle. Hold for 10–30 seconds at the highest point of tension, then switch legs.

TARGETS
- Hamstrings

BENEFITS
- Promotes myofascial release in the leg biceps

ANNOTATION KEY
Bold text indicates target muscles
Grey text indicates other working muscles
* indicates deep muscles

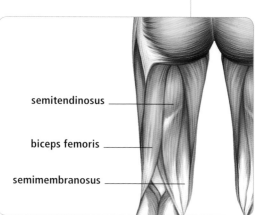

semitendinosus

biceps femoris

semimembranosus

ROLLING: GLUTES

1 Start in a seated position, with a foam roller placed directly beneath your glute muscles. Place your arms behind you for support.

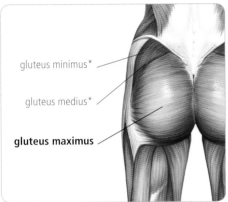

gluteus minimus*

gluteus medius*

gluteus maximus

ANNOTATION KEY

Bold text indicates target muscles

Grey text indicates other working muscles

* indicates deep muscles

2 Cross your right ankle over your left thigh, shifting your weight to one side.

TARGETS
• Glutes

BENEFITS
• Promotes myofascial release in the gluteus maximus

BEST FOR

• gluteus maximus

3 Begin rolling over the belly of the muscle. Hold for 10–30 seconds at the highest point of tension, then switch legs.

ROLLING: ILIOTIBIAL BAND

1 Lie facedown, supporting your weight on your hands, with your lower body slightly rotated so that your right leg rests on a foam roller situated between your knee and your hip. Cross your left leg over your right thigh; both feet should touch the floor. Keep as much of your weight on the bottom leg while relaxing the other.

2 Roll from your hip to your knee over the foam roller, and hold for 10–30 seconds at the point of greatest release. Switch legs and repeat.

TARGETS
• Iliotibial (IT) band

BENEFITS
• Promotes myofascial release in the iliotibial band

BEST FOR
• **tractus iliotibialis**

ANNOTATION KEY
Bold text indicates target muscles

Grey text indicates other working muscles

* indicates deep muscles

gluteus maximus

tractus iliotibialis

vastus lateralis

biceps femoris

semitendinosus

ROLLING: QUADRICEPS

1 Lie facedown, supporting your weight on your hands, with your lower body slightly rotated so that your right leg rests on a foam roller. The roller should be situated between your knee and your hip.

2 Keeping both legs and feet off the floor, roll over the area between your knee and your hip. Hold for 10–30 seconds at the highest point of tension, then switch legs.

BEST FOR

- vastus intermedius
- vastus lateralis
- vastus medialis
- rectus femoris

TARGETS
- Quadriceps

BENEFITS
- Promotes myofascial release in the quadriceps

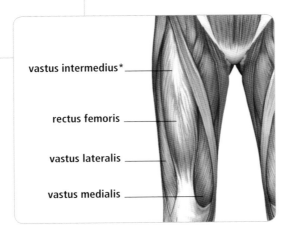

vastus intermedius*

rectus femoris

vastus lateralis

vastus medialis

ANNOTATION KEY
Bold text indicates target muscles
Grey text indicates other working muscles
* indicates deep muscles

19

ROLLING: LOWER BACK

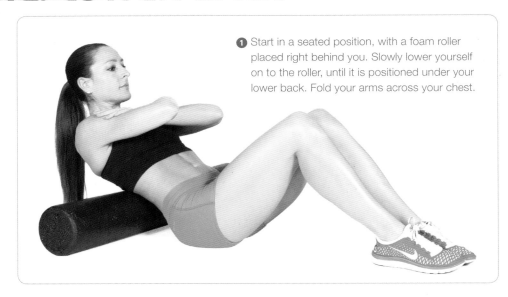

1 Start in a seated position, with a foam roller placed right behind you. Slowly lower yourself on to the roller, until it is positioned under your lower back. Fold your arms across your chest.

ANNOTATION KEY

Bold text indicates target muscles

Grey text indicates other working muscles

* indicates deep muscles

BEST FOR

• **erector spinae**

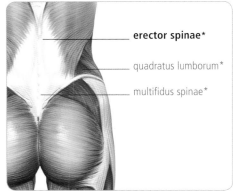

erector spinae*

quadratus lumborum*

multifidus spinae*

TARGETS
• Lower back

BENEFITS
• Promotes myofascial release in the erector spinae

2 Keeping your hips elevated and the tension on your lower back, slowly shift towards one side. Hold this position for 10–30 seconds, then repeat on the other side. Be sure to keep the weight on the muscles, not the spine.

STRETCHING: SHOULDERS

1 Begin in a standing position with your left arm lightly drawn across the front of your body.

2 Bring your right arm underneath your triceps, and gently pull your left arm across the front of your body. Hold for 10–30 seconds, then switch arms.

ANNOTATION KEY

Bold text indicates target muscles

Grey text indicates other working muscles

* indicates deep muscles

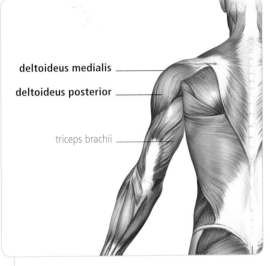

deltoideus medialis ————

deltoideus posterior ————

triceps brachii ————

BEST FOR

- **deltoideus posterior**
- **deltoideus medialis**

TARGETS
- Lateral and posterior deltoids

BENEFITS
- Increases flexibility, mobility, and performance in the upper body

STRETCHING: CHEST

BEST FOR

- pectoralis major
- pectoralis minor
- deltoideus anterior
- biceps brachii

1 Begin in a standing position, with your left arm drawn straight out to the side and your palm planted against a solid surface – a wall or doorframe, for example.

2 Keeping your feet planted on the floor and your left arm parallel to the ground, turn your upper body to the right, away from the wall, feeling a stretch across the chest. Hold for 10–30 seconds, then switch arms.

TARGETS
- Pectorals
- Anterior deltoids
- Biceps

BENEFITS
- Promotes flexibility in the chest, which is important for true upper body strength and mobility

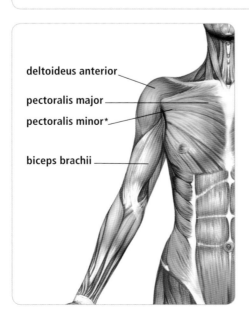

deltoideus anterior

pectoralis major

pectoralis minor*

biceps brachii

ANNOTATION KEY

Bold text indicates target muscles

Grey text indicates other working muscles

* indicates deep muscles

STRETCHING: LOWER BACK

❶ Lie on your back with your legs bent.

❷ Clasp your hands around your lower legs, and pull your knees towards your chest, feeling a deep stretch in the lower back. Hold for 10–30 seconds.

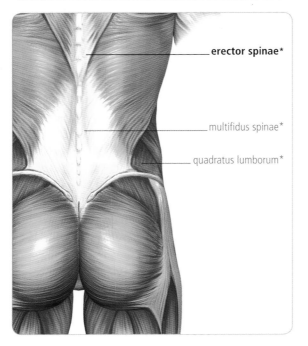

erector spinae*

multifidus spinae*

quadratus lumborum*

BEST FOR

- **erector spinae**

TARGETS
- Lower back

BENEFITS
- Promotes flexibility in the lower back, which is essential for mobility, injury prevention and performance

ANNOTATION KEY
Bold text indicates target muscles
Grey text indicates other working muscles
* indicates deep muscles

STRETCHING: GLUTES

1 Lie on your back, with your left leg bent and your foot firmly planted on the ground.

2 Cross your right ankle over the left thigh, resting it just above the kneecap.

BEST FOR

- gluteus maximus
- gluteus medius
- gluteus minimus

3 Reach between your legs to clasp your hands around the left leg and gently pull it towards you, feeling a stretch within the glutes. For a deeper stretch, lift your head off the floor. Hold for 10–30 seconds, then switch legs.

TARGETS
- Glutes

BENEFITS
- Improves the malleability of the gluteus maximus

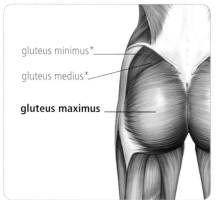

gluteus minimus*

gluteus medius*

gluteus maximus

ANNOTATION KEY

Bold text indicates target muscles

Grey text indicates other working muscles

* indicates deep muscles

STRETCHING: QUADRICEPS

❶ Begin in a standing position, then lift your left foot and bend your left leg behind you.

ANNOTATION KEY

Bold text indicates target muscles

Grey text indicates other working muscles

* indicates deep muscles

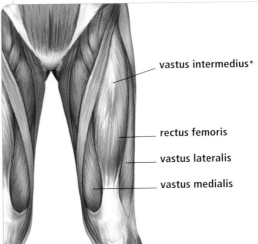

vastus intermedius*

rectus femoris

vastus lateralis

vastus medialis

BEST FOR

- **vastus intermedius**
- **vastus lateralis**
- **vastus medialis**
- **rectus femoris**

TARGETS
- Quadriceps

BENEFITS
- Promotes flexibility in the quadriceps, which is vital for optimal performance in the upper body

❷ Grab your raised foot with your left hand and pull it towards your upper thigh to feel a deep stretch within the quads. Hold for 10–30 seconds, then switch to the other side.

STRENGTH EXERCISES

In a strength exercise, muscles work together in compound movements — for example, the deadlift places emphasis on the lower back, with assistance from various leg and arm muscles.

The range of equipment used includes barbells, kettlebells, and bands. Barbells are, in a sense, the meat and potatoes of strength training, building unparalleled strength through the body. Kettlebells allow the body to work cohesively, drawing in ancillary helper muscles, as well as bringing balance and coordination into the lift. Bands allow for a different kind of stress that will allow you to work muscles from the inside out. By exploring and utilising all three of these training modes, you can create a body that is strong and resistant to breakdown.

BARBELL SQUATS

1 Begin standing in front of a barbell situated at eye level in a power rack. With your feet shoulder-width apart, duck beneath the barbell, so that it comes to rest across the back of your shoulders. Walk the barbell out of the rack.

TARGETS
- Thighs
- Glutes
- Core

BENEFITS
- Increases power and mass in the thighs

2 Inhale as you bend your knees, and lower yourself until your thighs are parallel to the ground. Be sure to keep your back flat as you do this.

3 Exhale as you push through your heels to stand erect. Perform 6–8 repetitions.

DO IT RIGHT
- Squat deep while keeping your thighs parallel to the ground.

AVOID
- Hyperextending your knees past your toes.

rectus abdominis

transversus abdominis*

vastus medialis

sartorius

adductor magnus

obliquus externus

obliquus internus*

vastus intermedius*

vastus lateralis

rectus femoris

ANNOTATION KEY

Bold text indicates target muscles

Grey text indicates other working muscles

* indicates deep muscles

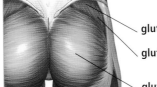

multifidus spinae*

gluteus minimus*

gluteus medius*

gluteus maximus

semitendinosus

biceps femoris

semimembranosus

BEST FOR

- vastus intermedius
- vastus lateralis
- vastus medialis
- rectus femoris
- semitendinosus
- biceps femoris
- semimembranosus
- gluteus maximus
- gluteus medius
- gluteus minimus

MODIFICATIONS

Easier: Complete the exercise as in the steps illustrated, but using your own body weight (right) instead of a barbell.

More difficult: Vary your foot stance. Bringing your feet closer together tends to increase the range of motion required, making the exercise more difficult.

BARBELL SQUAT SNATCH

1 Begin standing with your feet shoulder-width apart in front of a barbell. Squat down and grab the barbell with a wide overhand grip. Make sure your knees are close to the bar.

2 As you return to a standing position, flip the barbell directly overhead with your arms locked.

DO IT RIGHT
• Use your legs to help with the movement.

AVOID
• Overarching your back.

TARGETS
• Deltoids
• Thighs
• Glutes
• Upper back
• Core
• Triceps
• Hamstrings

BENEFITS
• Increases power and mass in the shoulders and thighs

3 Stand fully erect while holding the completed movement overhead.

4 Lower the barbell carefully to your chest and then down to the ground. Perform 6–8 repetitions.

BEST FOR

- deltoideus anterior
- deltoideus medialis
- deltoideus posterior
- vastus intermedius
- vastus lateralis
- vastus medialis
- rectus femoris
- gluteus maximus
- gluteus medius
- gluteus minimus

ANNOTATION KEY

Bold text indicates target muscles

Grey text indicates other working muscles

* indicates deep muscles

biceps brachii

triceps brachii

teres major

serratus anterior

latissimus dorsi

obliquus externus

tensor fasciae latae

rectus femoris

vastus lateralis

biceps femoris

deltoideus anterior

rectus abdominis

transversus abdominis*

adductor longus

sartorius

vastus intermedius*

vastus medialis

gracilis*

adductor magnus

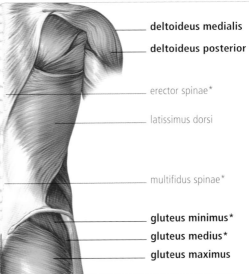

deltoideus medialis

deltoideus posterior

erector spinae*

latissimus dorsi

multifidus spinae*

gluteus minimus*

gluteus medius*

gluteus maximus

MODIFICATIONS

Easier: Execute the exercise using a very light barbell or just your own body weight.

More difficult: Use dumbbells (right) instead of a barbell.

BARBELL DEADLIFT

1 Begin standing with your feet shoulder-width apart in front of a barbell. Looking straight ahead, squat down and grab the barbell with a wide overhand grip; make sure your knees are close to the bar.

DO IT RIGHT
• Use your glutes to help with the movement.

AVOID
• Overarching your back.

TARGETS
• Erector spinae
• Quads
• Glutes
• Hamstrings
• Core
• Forearms
• Biceps

BENEFITS
• Increases power and mass in the torso

MODIFICATIONS
• **Easier:** Use a very light bar or just your own body weight.
• **More difficult:** Bring your feet closer together, since this increases the range of motion required, making the exercise more difficult.

2 Push through your heels as you stand erect while holding the barbell below you, at arms' length. Be sure to keep a straight back throughout this movement.

3 Stand fully erect while holding the completed movement, then carefully lower the barbell to the ground. Perform 6–8 repetitions.

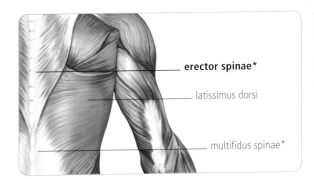

erector spinae*

latissimus dorsi

multifidus spinae*

ANNOTATION KEY

Bold text indicates target muscles

Grey text indicates other working muscles

* indicates deep muscles

BEST FOR

• erector spinae

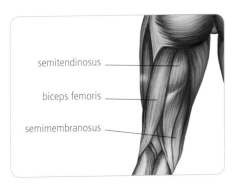

semitendinosus

biceps femoris

semimembranosus

deltoideus anterior

deltoideus medialis

deltoideus posterior

rectus abdominis

obliquus externus

gluteus maximus

brachioradialis

extensor digitorum

transversus abdominis*

biceps brachii

brachialis

flexor digitorum*

rectus femoris

vastus intermedius*

vastus medialis

sartorius

vastus lateralis

adductor longus

BENCH PRESS

❶ Lying on a bench, take an overhand shoulder-width grip on a barbell, and unrack it.

❷ Lower the bar through a slow, controlled movement to your nipple line, inhaling as you do so.

DO IT RIGHT
• Be sure to thrust your chest outward to complete the movement.

AVOID
• Bouncing the weight off your chest.

TARGETS
• Pectorals
• Anterior deltoids
• Triceps
• Abdominals
• Upper back

BENEFITS
• Increases power and mass in the chest

❸ Exhale as you push the bar to arms' length. Perform 6–8 repetitions.

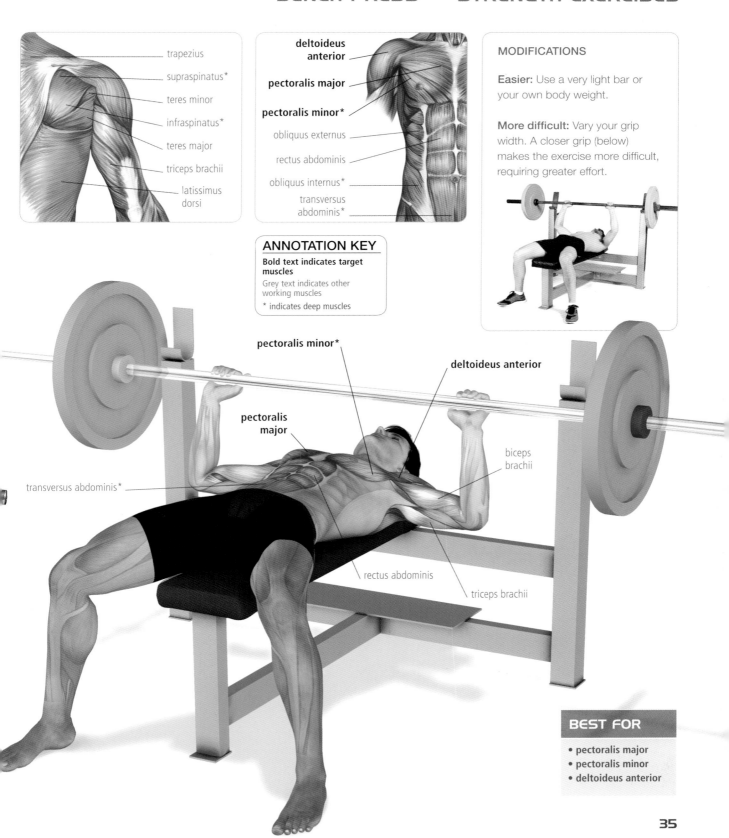

trapezius

supraspinatus*

teres minor

infraspinatus*

teres major

triceps brachii

latissimus dorsi

deltoideus anterior

pectoralis major

pectoralis minor*

obliquus externus

rectus abdominis

obliquus internus*

transversus abdominis*

ANNOTATION KEY

Bold text indicates target muscles

Grey text indicates other working muscles

* indicates deep muscles

MODIFICATIONS

Easier: Use a very light bar or your own body weight.

More difficult: Vary your grip width. A closer grip (below) makes the exercise more difficult, requiring greater effort.

pectoralis minor*

deltoideus anterior

pectoralis major

biceps brachii

transversus abdominis*

rectus abdominis

triceps brachii

BEST FOR

• pectoralis major
• pectoralis minor
• deltoideus anterior

BARBELL POWER CLEAN

DO IT RIGHT
• Be sure to use your legs to help with the movement.

AVOID
• Overarching your back.

❷ Straighten your legs to return to a standing position. As you do so, flip the bar until it is nearly touching your upper chest.

❶ Stand in front of a barbell with your feet shoulder-width apart. Looking straight ahead, squat down and grab the barbell with a wide overhand grip. Your knees should be close to the bar.

TARGETS
• Deltoids
• Upper back
• Thighs
• Glutes
• Hamstrings
• Core

BENEFITS
• Increases power and mass in the shoulders and upper back

❸ From the upper chest, reverse your flip and return to the starting position. Complete 6–8 repetitions.

MODIFICATIONS

Easier: Use a very light bar or just your own body weight.

More difficult: Use dumbbells instead of a barbell (right).

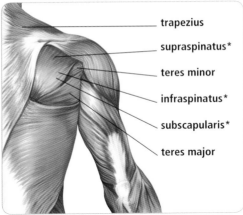

trapezius

supraspinatus*

teres minor

infraspinatus*

subscapularis*

teres major

ANNOTATION KEY

Bold text indicates target muscles

Grey text indicates other working muscles

* indicates deep muscles

BEST FOR

- **deltoideus anterior**
- **deltoideus medialis**
- **deltoideus posterior**
- **trapezius**
- **infraspinatus**
- **supraspinatus**
- **teres major**
- **teres minor**
- **subscapularis**

deltoideus anterior

deltoideus medialis

deltoideus posterior

latissimus dorsi

rectus abdominis

obliquus externus

gluteus maximus

biceps brachii

brachialis

extensor digitorum

anconeus

transversus abdominis*

vastus intermedius*

rectus femoris

vastus medialis

sartorius

adductor magnus

vastus lateralis

gluteus minimus*

gluteus medius*

gluteus maximus

semitendinosus

biceps femoris

semimembranosus

BARBELL POWER CLEAN AND JERK

1 Begin standing in front of a barbell; your feet should be shoulder-width apart. Squat down and grab the barbell with a wide overhand grip.

DO IT RIGHT
- Be sure to use your legs to help with the start of the movement.

AVOID
- Overarching your back.

2 As you return to a standing position, flip the barbell until it is nearly touching your upper chest.

TARGETS
- Deltoids
- Upper back
- Triceps
- Thighs
- Glutes
- Hamstrings
- Core

BENEFITS
- Increases power and mass in the shoulders and upper back

MODIFICATIONS

Easier: Use a very light bar or just your own body weight.

More difficult: Use dumbbells (below) instead of a barbell.

3 Next, push the barbell overhead, holding it at arms' length.

4 Lower the barbell back to your upper chest, reverse your flip, and return it to the floor. Perform 6–8 repetitions.

BEST FOR

- deltoideus anterior
- deltoideus medialis
- deltoideus posterior
- trapezius
- supraspinatus
- infraspinatus
- teres major
- erector spinae
- rhomboideus
- triceps brachii

ANNOTATION KEY

Bold text indicates target muscles
Grey text indicates other working muscles
* indicates deep muscles

brachialis

biceps brachii

teres major

serratus anterior

latissimus dorsi

obliquus externus

tractus iliotibialis

tensor fasciae latae

vastus lateralis

rectus femoris

triceps brachii

deltoideus medialis

deltoideus anterior

rectus abdominis

transversus abdominis*

adductor longus

vastus intermedius*

sartorius

vastus medialis

gracilis*

adductor magnus

trapezius

deltoideus posterior

supraspinatus*

infraspinatus*

teres major

rhomboideus*

erector spinae*

STANDING BARBELL PRESS

❶ Stand in front of a barbell, situated at eye level in a power rack. Grab the barbell with an overhand grip that is shoulder-width apart and walk back with it.

DO IT RIGHT
- Always press to the front of the shoulders – never behind your neck.

AVOID
- Leaning back excessively.

TARGETS
- Deltoids
- Triceps
- Upper back
- Core

BENEFITS
- Increases power and mass in the shoulders and upper arms

MODIFICATIONS

Easier: Use a very light bar or just your own body weight.

More difficult: Use dumbbells (below) instead of a barbell.

❷ Extend your arms, pushing the barbell overhead, from your upper chest to arms' length.

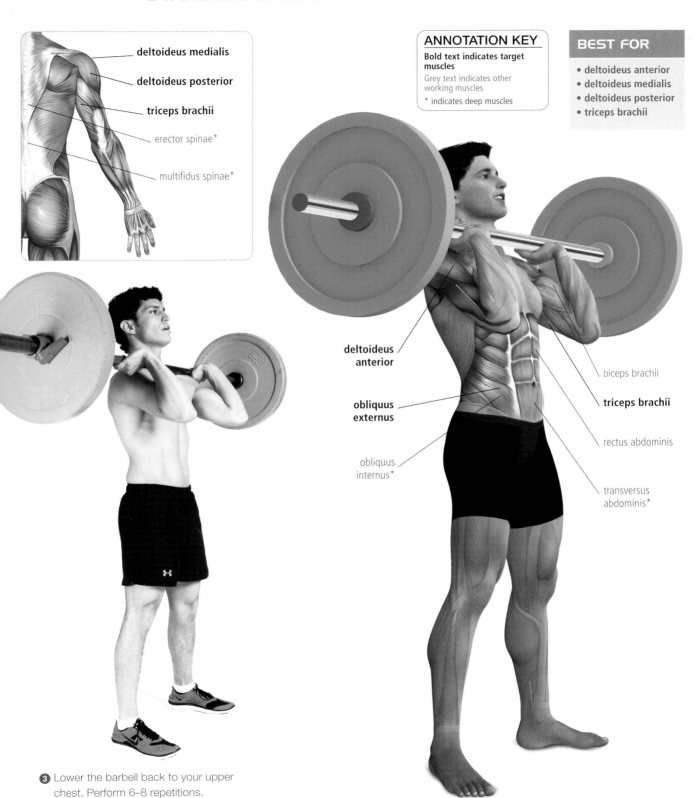

deltoideus medialis

deltoideus posterior

triceps brachii

erector spinae*

multifidus spinae*

ANNOTATION KEY

Bold text indicates target muscles

Grey text indicates other working muscles

* indicates deep muscles

BEST FOR

• deltoideus anterior
• deltoideus medialis
• deltoideus posterior
• triceps brachii

deltoideus anterior

obliquus externus

obliquus internus*

biceps brachii

triceps brachii

rectus abdominis

transversus abdominis*

3 Lower the barbell back to your upper chest. Perform 6–8 repetitions.

BARBELL SHOULDER SHRUG

1 Pick up a barbell and let it hang at arms' length in front of you.

DO IT RIGHT
• Always shrug straight up and down.

AVOID
• Rolling your shoulders backwards.

2 Shrug your shoulders up, bringing them as close to your ears as possible.

TARGETS
• Trapezius
• Neck
• Upper back
• Forearms
• Core

BENEFITS
• Increases power and mass in the trapezius muscles

3 Return to the starting position. Complete 10–12 repetitions.

sternocleidomastoideus

trapezius

palmaris longus

obliquus externus

flexor digitorum*

rectus abdominis

transversus abdominis*

extensor carpi radialis

splenius*

levator scapulae*

supraspinatus*

infraspinatus*

teres major

rhomboideus*

trapezius

erector spinae*

ANNOTATION KEY

Bold text indicates target muscles

Grey text indicates other working muscles

* indicates deep muscles

BEST FOR

- trapezius
- splenius
- levator scapulae
- supraspinatus
- infraspinatus
- teres major
- rhomboideus
- erector spinae

MODIFICATIONS

Easier: Try using a very light bar instead of a barbell.

More difficult: Use dumbbells (right) instead of a barbell.

BARBELL UPRIGHT ROWS

1 Pick up a barbell with a relatively close grip and let it hang at arms' length in front of you.

2 Keeping your body erect, pull the barbell straight up.

TARGETS
- Front deltoids
- Trapezius
- Upper back
- Forearms
- Biceps
- Core

BENEFITS
- Increases power and mass in the trapezius muscles

3 When the barbell is nearly touching your chin, lower it back to arms' length. Repeat 10–12 times.

DO IT RIGHT
- Always keep the barbell close to your body, and lead with your elbows.

AVOID
- Hitting your chin with the barbell.

trapezius

supraspinatus*

infraspinatus*

teres major

rhomboideus*

deltoideus medialis

sternocleidomastoideus

trapezius

deltoideus anterior

biceps brachii

palmaris longus

serratus anterior

rectus abdominis

obliquus externus

transversus abdominis*

ANNOTATION KEY

Bold text indicates target muscles

Grey text indicates other working muscles

* indicates deep muscles

MODIFICATIONS

Easier: Use a very light bar instead of a barbell.

More difficult: Use a wider grip on the barbell (below).

BEST FOR

- deltoideus anterior
- trapezius

DUMBBELL PULLOVER

❶ Lie on a flat bench with your head supported. Bend your legs and place your feet, shoulder-width apart, flat on the bench for extra lower-back support.

❷ Hold a light dumbbell above your chest with your arms extended.

DO IT RIGHT
• Always bend your arms when performing this exercise.

AVOID
• Hitting your head with the dumbbell.

TARGETS
• Serratus
• Latissimus dorsi
• Pectorals
• Triceps
• Core

BENEFITS
• Increases both mass and range of motion in the latissimus dorsi

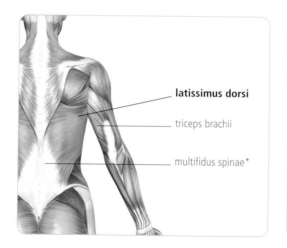

latissimus dorsi

triceps brachii

multifidus spinae*

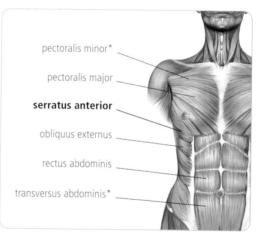

pectoralis minor*

pectoralis major

serratus anterior

obliquus externus

rectus abdominis

transversus abdominis*

MODIFICATIONS

Easier: Use a very light dumbbell.

More difficult: Lay across a bench with only your head and shoulders supported (right).

BEST FOR
• serratus anterior
• latissimus dorsi

ANNOTATION KEY
Bold text indicates target muscles
Grey text indicates other working muscles
* indicates deep muscles

3 Bend your arms as you move the dumbbell well behind your head, then extend them back up as you return to the starting position. Complete 8–10 repetitions.

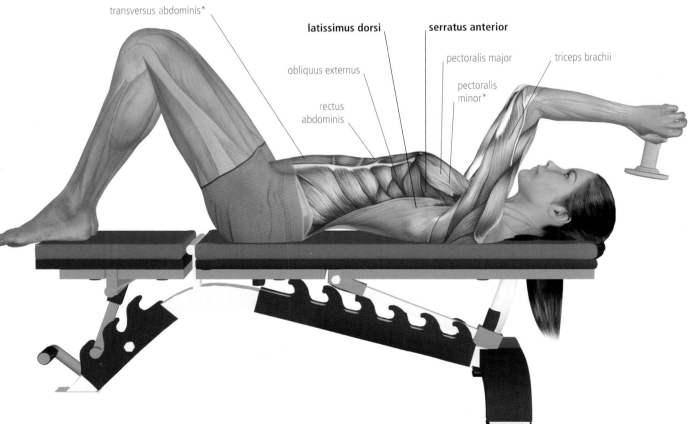

transversus abdominis*

latissimus dorsi

serratus anterior

obliquus externus

pectoralis major

triceps brachii

pectoralis minor*

rectus abdominis

DIPS

STRENGTH EXERCISES

① Begin standing in front of a dip station or parallel bars.

DO IT RIGHT
- Always complete a full range of motion.

AVOID
- Performing the exercise at excessive speed.

② Place one hand on each bar, and grip as you push and extend your arms to full lockout.

TARGETS
- Pectorals
- Triceps
- Upper back
- Forearms
- Core

BENEFITS
- Increases strength and mass in the upper body

MODIFICATIONS
- **Easier:** Have a partner support the weight of your legs.
- **More difficult:** Place a dumbbell between your lower legs for increased resistance.

③ Lower yourself until your upper arms are parallel to the ground, then push back up to the starting position. Complete 8–10 repetitions.

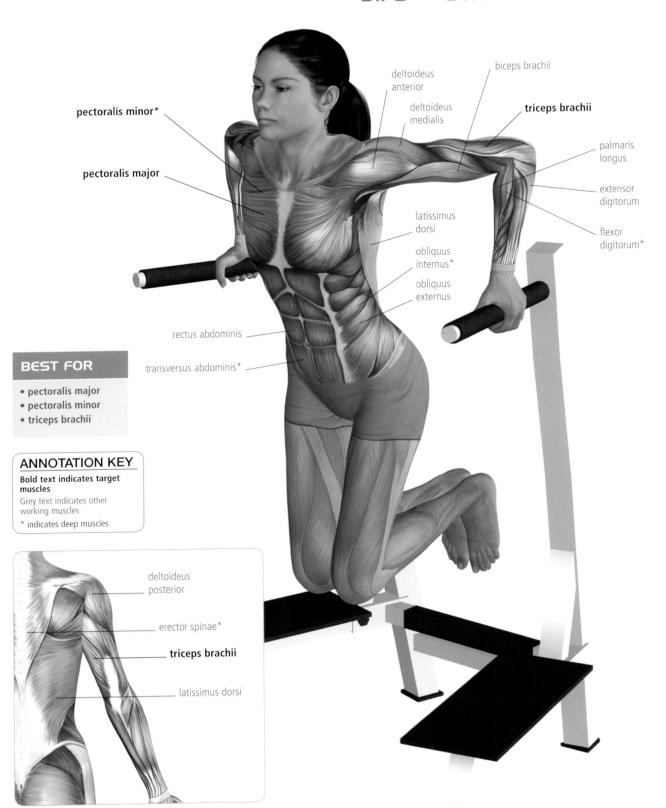

pectoralis minor*

pectoralis major

deltoideus anterior

deltoideus medialis

biceps brachii

triceps brachii

palmaris longus

extensor digitorum

flexor digitorum*

latissimus dorsi

obliquus internus*

obliquus externus

rectus abdominis

transversus abdominis*

BEST FOR

- **pectoralis major**
- **pectoralis minor**
- **triceps brachii**

ANNOTATION KEY

Bold text indicates target muscles

Grey text indicates other working muscles

* indicates deep muscles

deltoideus posterior

erector spinae*

triceps brachii

latissimus dorsi

WIDE-GRIP HIGH PULL

① Stand in front of a barbell with your feet hip-width apart; your shins should be close to the bar.

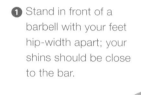

② Bend your legs until your thighs are nearly parallel to the ground, then grab the barbell with a grip that is just beyond shoulder-width.

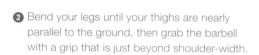

③ Keeping a flat back, straighten your knees to stand up, then pull the barbell up to your shoulders.

TARGETS
- Legs
- Upper back
- Forearms
- Core

BENEFITS
- Increases both strength and mass in the upper body and thighs

MODIFICATIONS
- **Easier:** Use a lighter barbell.
- **More difficult:** Vary your foot stance. Bringing your feet closer together tends to increase the range of motion required, making the exercise more difficult.

DO IT RIGHT
- Always keep a flat back.

AVOID
- Performing the exercise at excessive speed.

④ Lower the barbell to arms' length and return it to the floor. Perform 8–10 repetitions.

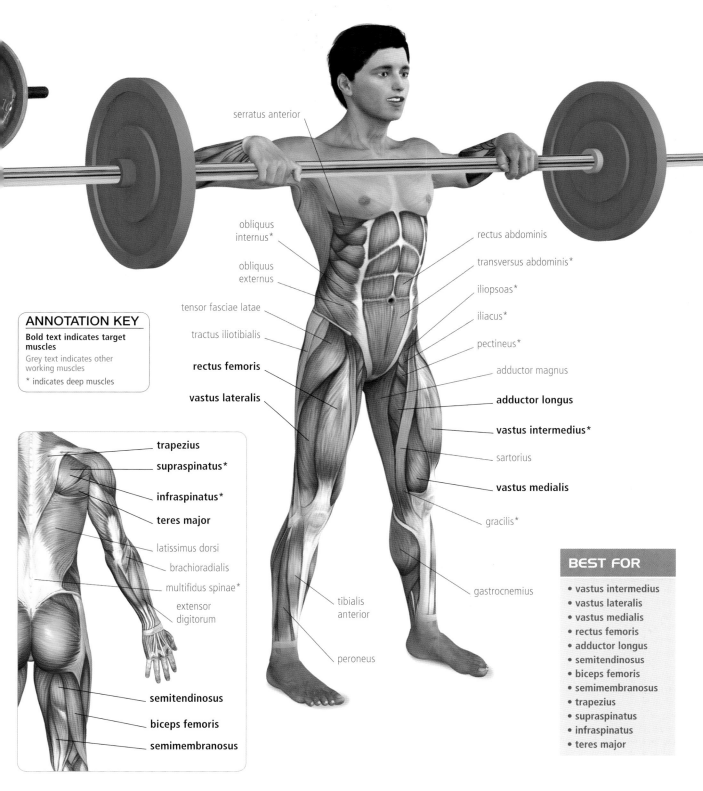

serratus anterior

obliquus internus*

obliquus externus

tensor fasciae latae

tractus iliotibialis

rectus femoris

vastus lateralis

rectus abdominis

transversus abdominis*

iliopsoas*

iliacus*

pectineus*

adductor magnus

adductor longus

vastus intermedius*

sartorius

vastus medialis

gracilis*

gastrocnemius

tibialis anterior

peroneus

ANNOTATION KEY

Bold text indicates target muscles

Grey text indicates other working muscles

* indicates deep muscles

trapezius

supraspinatus*

infraspinatus*

teres major

latissimus dorsi

brachioradialis

multifidus spinae*

extensor digitorum

semitendinosus

biceps femoris

semimembranosus

BEST FOR

- vastus intermedius
- vastus lateralis
- vastus medialis
- rectus femoris
- adductor longus
- semitendinosus
- biceps femoris
- semimembranosus
- trapezius
- supraspinatus
- infraspinatus
- teres major

51

REVERSE CLOSE-GRIP FRONT CHIN

DO IT RIGHT
• Always perform a full range of motion.

AVOID
• Dropping your body weight suddenly.

TARGETS
• Lower latissimus dorsi
• Forearms
• Biceps

BENEFITS
• Increases both strength and width in the back muscles

MODIFICATIONS
• **Easier:** Have a partner assist you by supporting the weight of your legs.
• **More difficult:** Place a dumbbell between your lower legs for increased resistance.

❶ Standing in front of a pull-up bar, either reach up or step on a stool. Take an underhand close grip and hang below at arms' length.

❷ Cross your legs at the ankles, and pull yourself up.

❸ When your chin is as close to the bar as possible, lower yourself back to arms' length. Repeat 8–10 times.

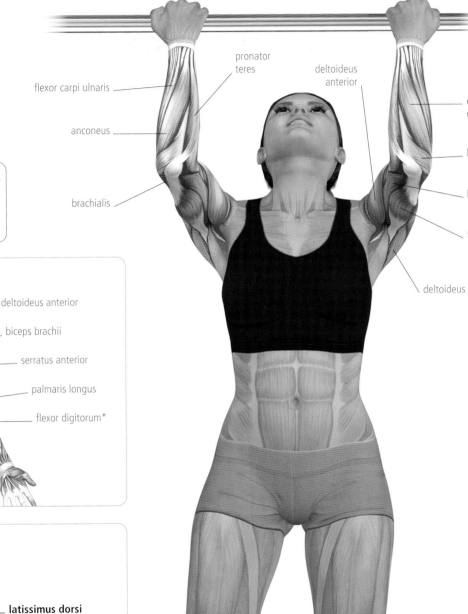

BEST FOR

• latissimus dorsi

ANNOTATION KEY

Bold text indicates target muscles

Grey text indicates other working muscles

* indicates deep muscles

pronator teres

flexor carpi ulnaris

anconeus

brachialis

deltoideus anterior

extensor digitorum

brachioradialis

biceps brachii

triceps brachii

deltoideus posterior

deltoideus anterior

biceps brachii

serratus anterior

palmaris longus

flexor digitorum*

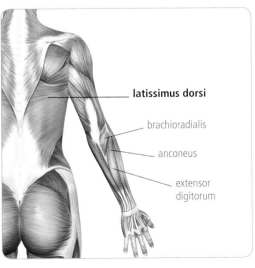

latissimus dorsi

brachioradialis

anconeus

extensor digitorum

LAT PULLDOWNS

1 Begin in a seated position at the pulldown machine. Grab the bar with an overhand grip that is slightly wider than shoulder-width.

2 Pull the bar down to the very top of your chest.

TARGETS
• Latissimus dorsi
• Forearms
• Biceps

BENEFITS
• Increases both strength and width in the back muscles

MODIFICATIONS
• **Easier:** Try using a wider grip to reduce your range of motion.
• **More difficult:** A closer grip will increase your range of motion, making the exercise harder.

3 Fully extend your arms overhead using a controlled movement. Complete 8–10 repetitions.

DO IT RIGHT
• Always sit up straight, maintaining a flat back.

AVOID
• Pulling the bar behind your neck.

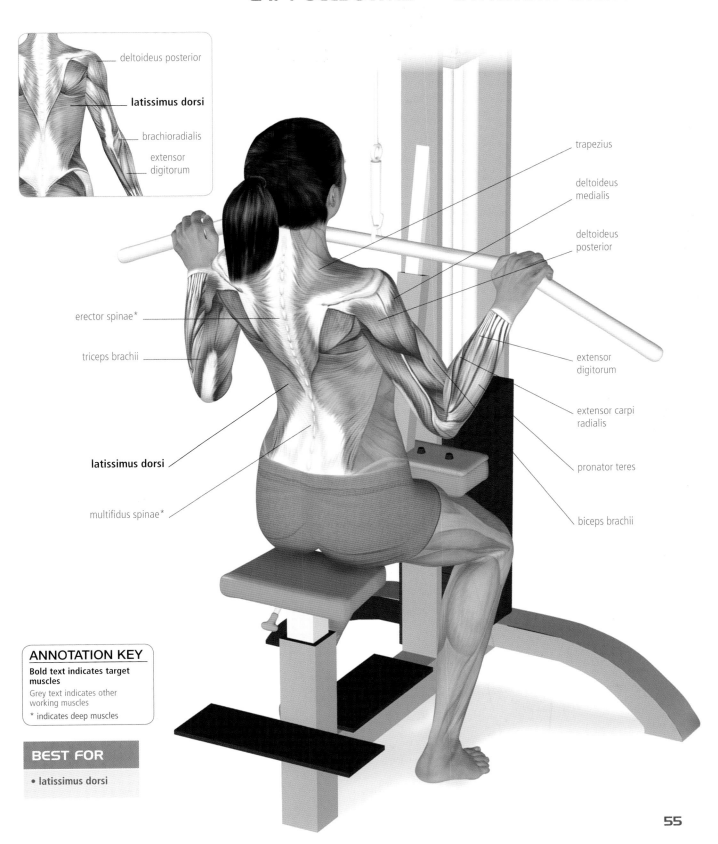

deltoideus posterior

latissimus dorsi

brachioradialis

extensor digitorum

trapezius

deltoideus medialis

deltoideus posterior

erector spinae*

triceps brachii

extensor digitorum

extensor carpi radialis

latissimus dorsi

pronator teres

multifidus spinae*

biceps brachii

ANNOTATION KEY

Bold text indicates target muscles

Grey text indicates other working muscles

* indicates deep muscles

BEST FOR

• latissimus dorsi

BARBELL CURL

1 Begin in a standing position, holding a barbell at arms' length, with an underhand grip shoulder-width apart.

2 Keeping your elbows in at your sides, bend the arms and bring the palms of your hands towards your chest.

TARGETS
- Biceps
- Forearms
- Core

BENEFITS
- Increases both strength and mass in the biceps

3 When the barbell is close to your collarbone, lower it. Repeat 8–10 times.

DO IT RIGHT
- Always employ a full range of motion.

AVOID
- Swinging the barbell up using your back.

56

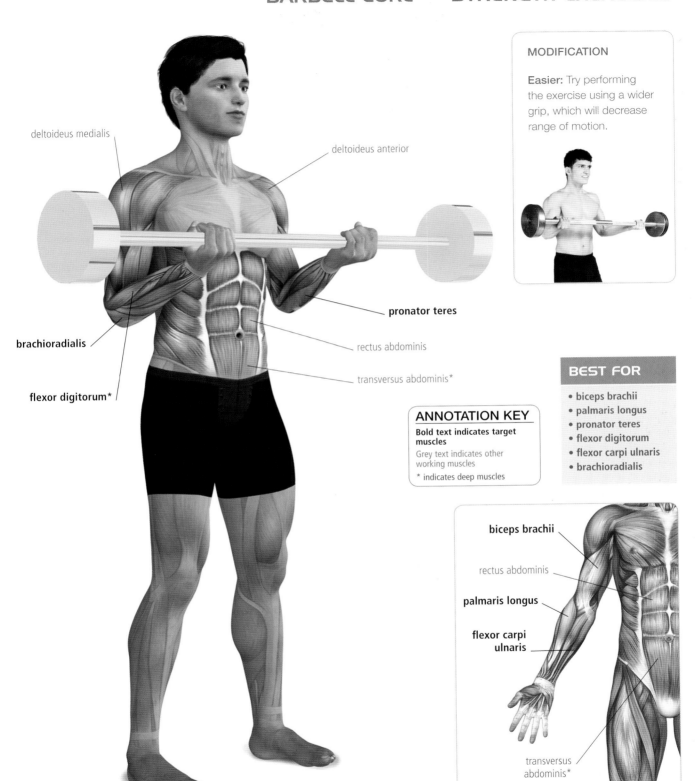

deltoideus medialis

deltoideus anterior

brachioradialis

flexor digitorum*

pronator teres

rectus abdominis

transversus abdominis*

MODIFICATION

Easier: Try performing the exercise using a wider grip, which will decrease range of motion.

ANNOTATION KEY

Bold text indicates target muscles

Grey text indicates other working muscles

* indicates deep muscles

BEST FOR

- biceps brachii
- palmaris longus
- pronator teres
- flexor digitorum
- flexor carpi ulnaris
- brachioradialis

biceps brachii

rectus abdominis

palmaris longus

flexor carpi ulnaris

transversus abdominis*

GOBLET SQUAT

DO IT RIGHT
- Always employ a full range of motion.

AVOID
- Hyperextending your knees past your toes.

TARGETS
- Quadriceps
- Calves
- Glutes
- Hamstrings
- Shoulders

BENEFITS
- Helps build strength in the quadriceps

MODIFICATIONS
- **Easier:** A wider stance will reduce range of motion.
- **More difficult:** A closer stance will increase range of motion.

1 While in a standing position, hold a kettlebell with both hands close to your chest. Your legs should be a little more than shoulder-width apart, with your toes pointing slightly outwards.

2 Squat down until your thighs are parallel to the floor, bringing your elbows to your thighs.

3 Keep your back flat as you push through your heels back to the standing position. Complete 8–10 repetitions.

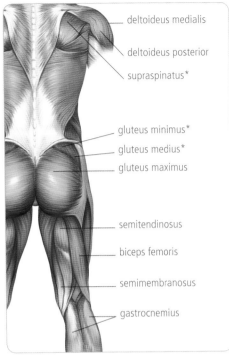

deltoideus medialis

deltoideus posterior

supraspinatus*

gluteus minimus*

gluteus medius*

gluteus maximus

semitendinosus

biceps femoris

semimembranosus

gastrocnemius

ANNOTATION KEY

Bold text indicates target muscles

Grey text indicates other working muscles

* indicates deep muscles

BEST FOR

- **vastus intermedius**
- **vastus lateralis**
- **vastus medialis**
- **rectus femoris**

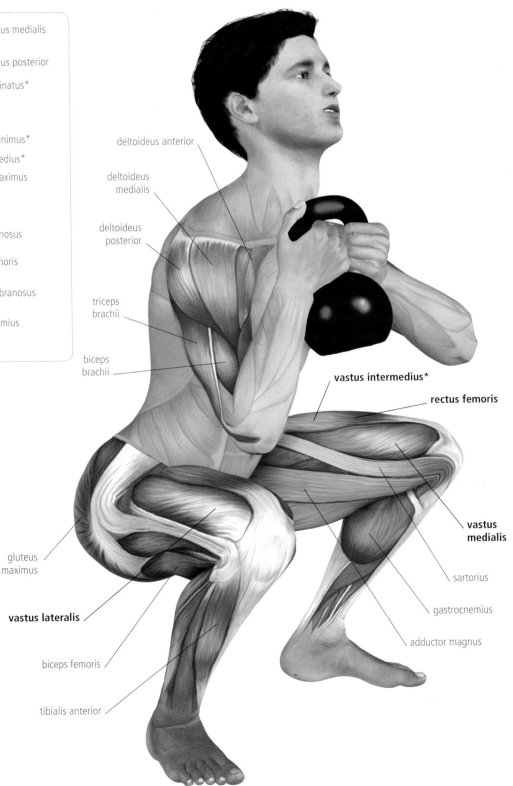

deltoideus anterior

deltoideus medialis

deltoideus posterior

triceps brachii

biceps brachii

vastus intermedius*

rectus femoris

vastus medialis

sartorius

gastrocnemius

adductor magnus

gluteus maximus

vastus lateralis

biceps femoris

tibialis anterior

ONE-ARM KETTLEBELL CLEAN

① Take a standing position, with your feet shoulder-width apart and knees slightly bent, holding a kettlebell in one hand.

TARGETS
- Hamstrings
- Glutes
- Lower back
- Shoulders
- Trapezius

BENEFITS
- Helps build strength in the hamstrings

MODIFICATIONS
- **Easier:** A wider stance reduces range of motion.
- **More difficult:** A closer stance will increase your range of motion.

DO IT RIGHT
- Work cohesively with your opposing muscles.

AVOID
- Using excessive momentum when cleaning the kettlebell to your shoulder.

② Bend down as you push your rear out behind you with your eyes looking straight ahead.

③ Clean the kettlebell to your shoulder by rotating the wrist and extending through the legs and hips. Return to the starting position. Complete 8–10 repetitions per arm.

BEST FOR

- semitendinosus
- biceps femoris
- semimembranosus

ANNOTATION KEY

Bold text indicates target muscles

Grey text indicates other working muscles

* indicates deep muscles

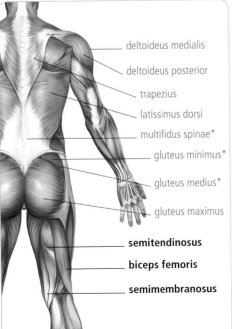

deltoideus medialis

deltoideus posterior

trapezius

latissimus dorsi

multifidus spinae*

gluteus minimus*

gluteus medius*

gluteus maximus

semitendinosus

biceps femoris

semimembranosus

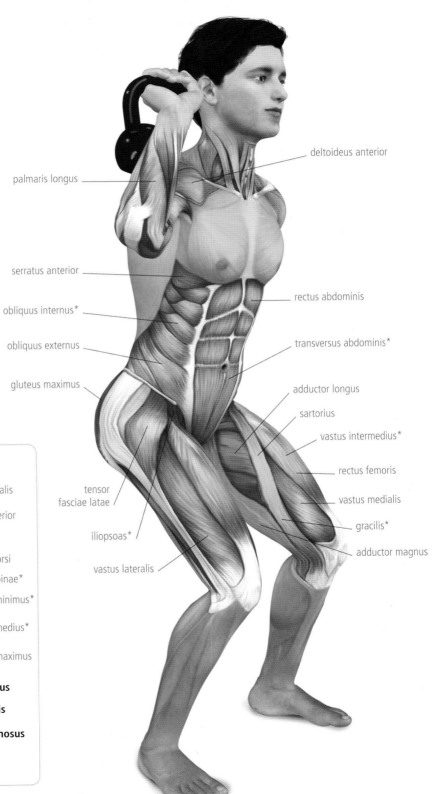

palmaris longus

deltoideus anterior

serratus anterior

rectus abdominis

obliquus internus*

obliquus externus

transversus abdominis*

gluteus maximus

adductor longus

sartorius

vastus intermedius*

rectus femoris

tensor fasciae latae

vastus medialis

iliopsoas*

gracilis*

adductor magnus

vastus lateralis

ALTERNATING KETTLEBELL ROW

❶ Stand upright with your feet shoulder-width apart. Hold a pair of kettlebells in front of you with an overhand grip. Bend forwards slightly at the waist, maintaining a flat back.

❷ Bend your arm at the elbow, and pull your left hand up towards your abdomen, then lower it again.

DO IT RIGHT
• Maintain a flat back during the exercise.

AVOID
• Rotating your core.

TARGETS
• Middle back
• Biceps
• Latissimus dorsi

BENEFITS
• Builds strength in the middle back

MODIFICATIONS

Easier: Lift with both arms at the same time (below).

More difficult: Raise one leg off the floor for a tougher challenge.

❸ Next, pull your right hand up, then lower it. Complete 8–10 repetitions per hand.

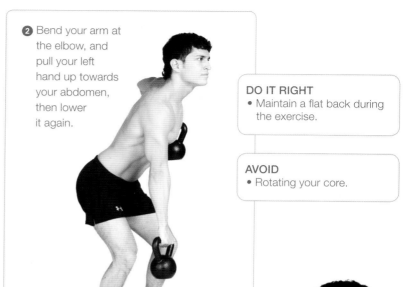

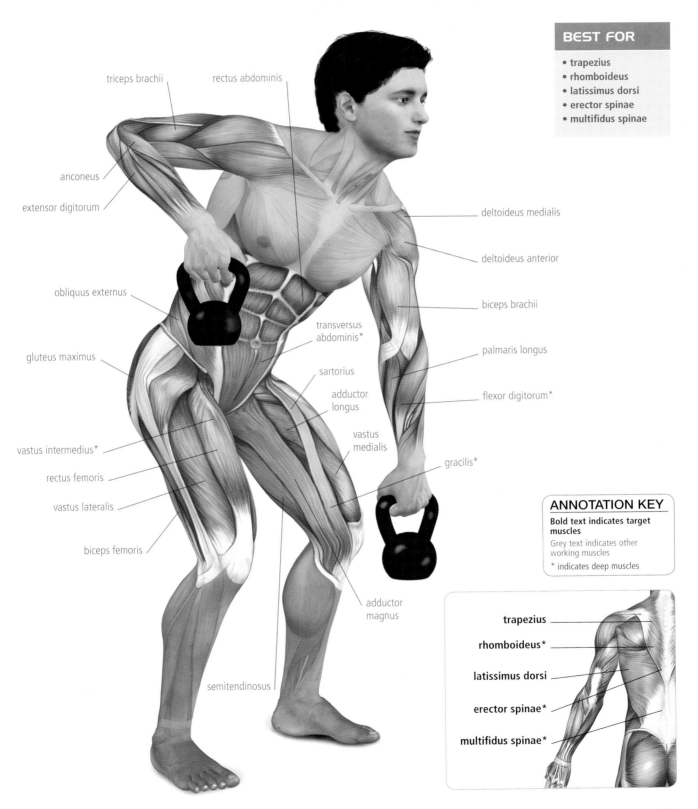

BEST FOR

- trapezius
- rhomboideus
- latissimus dorsi
- erector spinae
- multifidus spinae

triceps brachii

rectus abdominis

anconeus

extensor digitorum

obliquus externus

gluteus maximus

vastus intermedius*

rectus femoris

vastus lateralis

biceps femoris

semitendinosus

deltoideus medialis

deltoideus anterior

biceps brachii

transversus abdominis*

sartorius

adductor longus

palmaris longus

flexor digitorum*

vastus medialis

gracilis*

adductor magnus

ANNOTATION KEY

Bold text indicates target muscles

Grey text indicates other working muscles

* indicates deep muscles

trapezius

rhomboideus*

latissimus dorsi

erector spinae*

multifidus spinae*

63

ALTERNATING RENEGADE ROW

❶ With a kettlebell in each hand, plant yourself
on the floor in a push-up position.

DO IT RIGHT
- Keep your core stable and
straight on.

TARGETS
- Middle back
- Abdominals
- Biceps
- Chest
- Latissimus dorsi
- Triceps

BENEFITS
- Builds strength in
the middle back

AVOID
- Dropping or slamming the
weight into the floor.

❷ While staying up on your toes and
keeping your core stable and parallel
to the floor, pull the kettlebell in your
right hand up towards your chest while
straightening the left arm and pushing
that kettlebell into the floor.

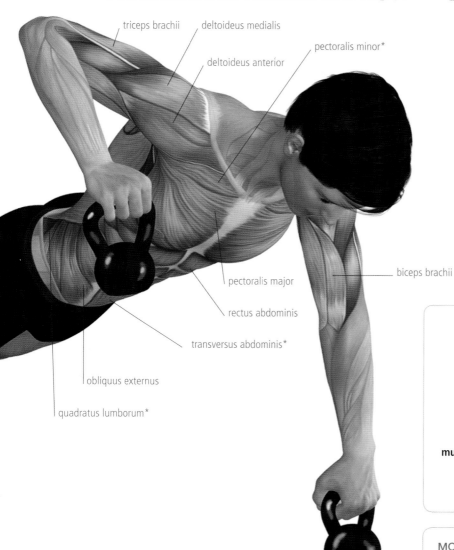

triceps brachii

deltoideus medialis

pectoralis minor*

deltoideus anterior

biceps brachii

pectoralis major

rectus abdominis

transversus abdominis*

obliquus externus

quadratus lumborum*

BEST FOR

- **trapezius**
- **rhomboideus**
- **latissimus dorsi**
- **erector spinae**
- **multifidus spinae**

ANNOTATION KEY

Bold text indicates target muscles

Grey text indicates other working muscles

* indicates deep muscles

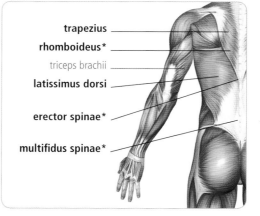

trapezius

rhomboideus*

triceps brachii

latissimus dorsi

erector spinae*

multifidus spinae*

MODIFICATIONS

Easier: Row with just one kettlebell while keeping the empty hand planted flat on the floor. Switch hands after 10 repetitions.

More difficult: Raise one leg off the floor (below) for a tougher challenge.

3 Lower your right arm, then repeat the movement with the left. Complete 8–10 repetitions per arm.

STRENGTH EXERCISES

DO IT RIGHT
• Keep your core engaged and straight on.

AVOID
• Leaning back too far when executing the movement.

TARGETS
• Deltoids
• Triceps

BENEFITS
• Builds strength in the shoulder

❶ Stand with your feet shoulder-width apart and a pair of kettlebells cleaned to the sides of your shoulders. Your palms should be facing each other.

❷ Raise the right kettlebell directly overhead until your arm locks out, turning the palm forwards in mid-motion. Keep the other kettlebell as still as possible.

MODIFICATIONS

Easier: Press with both arms at the same time (right).

More difficult: Raise one leg off the floor for a tougher challenge.

deltoideus posterior

deltoideus medialis

triceps brachii

ANNOTATION KEY

Bold text indicates target muscles

Grey text indicates other working muscles

* indicates deep muscles

triceps brachii

deltoideus anterior

pectoralis minor*

pectoralis major

pronator teres

obliquus externus

obliquus internus*

quadratus lumborum*

BEST FOR

- **deltoideus anterior**
- **deltoideus posterior**
- **deltoideus medialis**

❸ Lower your right arm, turning the palm back towards you as you do so, then complete the same movement with the left. Perform 8–10 repetitions per arm.

DOUBLE KETTLEBELL SNATCH

DO IT RIGHT
• Keep your back straight throughout the movement.

AVOID
• Powering through the movement and overusing your shoulders.

TARGETS
• Deltoids
• Glutes
• Quads
• Hamstrings

BENEFITS
• Builds strength in the shoulders

MODIFICATIONS
• **Easier:** Use just one kettlebell and lift it with both hands.
• **More difficult:** Alternate the arms, so you lift one kettlebell at a time.

1 Stand with your feet a little more than shoulder-width apart, holding a pair of kettlebells at your sides.

2 Squat down, leaning forwards slightly and sticking out your behind. Bring your arms between your legs, so that the kettlebells are next to your inner thighs.

3 In one swift and determined movement, drive through your hips and swing the kettlebells overhead. Lower and repeat 8–10 times.

BEST FOR

- deltoideus anterior
- deltoideus medialis
- deltoideus posterior

ANNOTATION KEY

Bold text indicates target muscles

Grey text indicates other working muscles

* indicates deep muscles

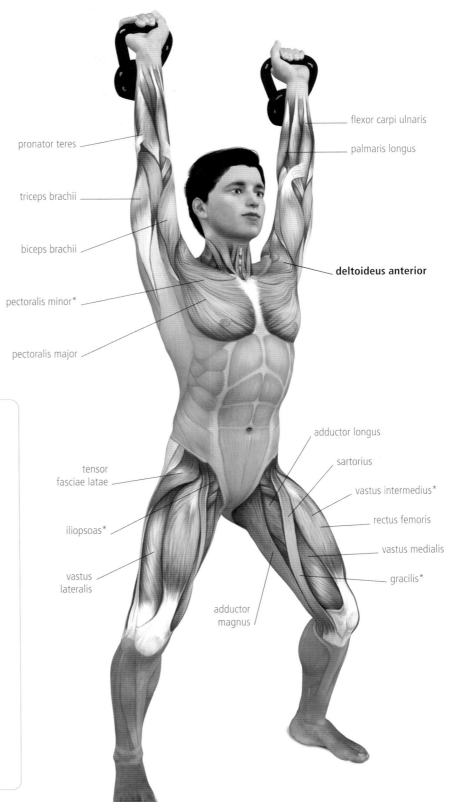

pronator teres

flexor carpi ulnaris

palmaris longus

triceps brachii

biceps brachii

deltoideus anterior

pectoralis minor*

pectoralis major

adductor longus

sartorius

tensor fasciae latae

vastus intermedius*

rectus femoris

iliopsoas*

vastus medialis

vastus lateralis

gracilis*

adductor magnus

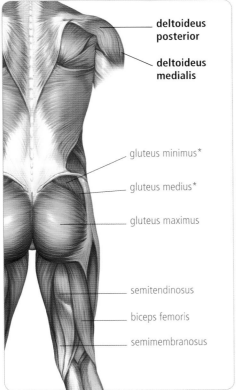

deltoideus posterior

deltoideus medialis

gluteus minimus*

gluteus medius*

gluteus maximus

semitendinosus

biceps femoris

semimembranosus

PLYO KETTLEBELL PUSH-UP

1 Assume a classic push-up position, on your toes, with one hand planted on the floor and the other gripping a kettlebell. Lower yourself until your upper arms are parallel to the floor.

DO IT RIGHT
- Keep your back flat throughout the movement.

AVOID
- Bouncing excessively and using momentum.

2 Next, quickly push your arms to full extension. As you do so, switch hands on the kettlebell.

TARGETS
- Pectorals
- Shoulders
- Triceps

BENEFITS
- Builds strength in the chest

3 Lower yourself again, switching sides each time you push yourself back up. Complete 8–10 push-ups per side.

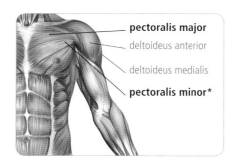

pectoralis major

deltoideus anterior

deltoideus medialis

pectoralis minor*

MODIFICATIONS

Easier: Keep the same hand planted on the kettlebell.

More difficult: Perform the push-ups with both hands gripping kettlebells (right).

ANNOTATION KEY

Bold text indicates target muscles

Grey text indicates other working muscles

* indicates deep muscles

BEST FOR

- **pectoralis major**
- **pectoralis minor**

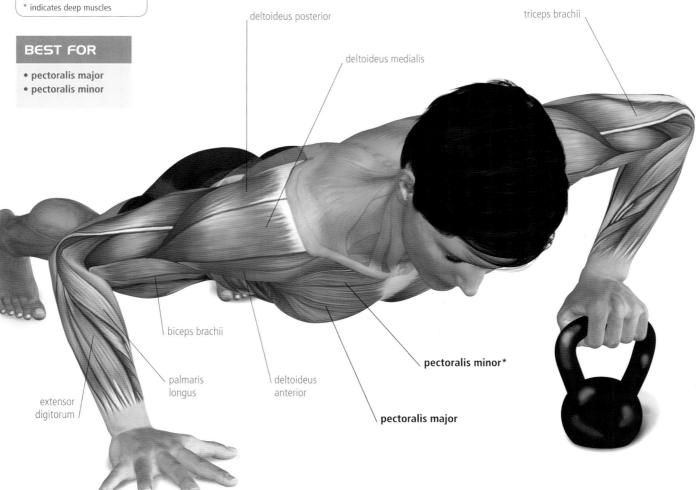

deltoideus posterior

triceps brachii

deltoideus medialis

biceps brachii

pectoralis minor*

palmaris longus

deltoideus anterior

extensor digitorum

pectoralis major

ADVANCED KETTLEBELL WINDMILL

DO IT RIGHT
• Keep your back flat throughout the movement.

AVOID
• Bouncing excessively and using momentum.

① With your right arm by your side and your feet shoulder-width apart, stand with a kettlebell in your left hand, raised overhead.

TARGETS
• Abdominals
• Glutes
• Hamstrings
• Shoulders

BENEFITS
• Increases strength in the abdominals

② Push your left hip out to the left and slightly bend your knees while lowering your torso to the right as far as possible. Pause, then return to the starting position. Complete 8–10 repetitions per side.

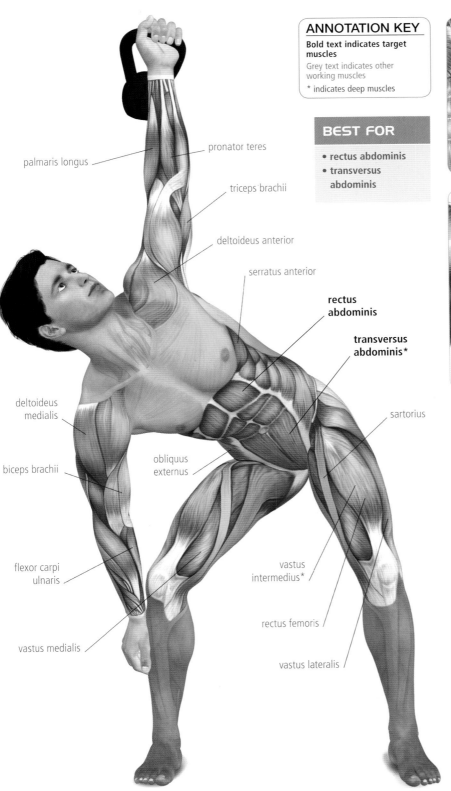

palmaris longus

pronator teres

triceps brachii

deltoideus anterior

serratus anterior

rectus abdominis

transversus abdominis*

deltoideus medialis

biceps brachii

obliquus externus

flexor carpi ulnaris

vastus medialis

sartorius

vastus intermedius*

rectus femoris

vastus lateralis

ANNOTATION KEY

Bold text indicates target muscles

Grey text indicates other working muscles

* indicates deep muscles

BEST FOR

- rectus abdominis
- transversus abdominis

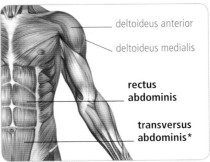

deltoideus anterior

deltoideus medialis

rectus abdominis

transversus abdominis*

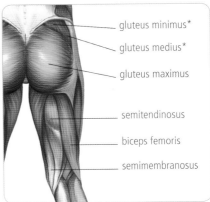

gluteus minimus*

gluteus medius*

gluteus maximus

semitendinosus

biceps femoris

semimembranosus

MODIFICATION

Easier: Perform the exercise without holding a kettlebell.

KETTLEBELL FIGURE 8

DO IT RIGHT
- Keep your back flat throughout the movement.

AVOID
- Bouncing excessively and relying on momentum.

❶ Assume a wide stance and hold a kettlebell in your right hand, between your legs, close to your right thigh. Bend forwards slightly, keeping your back flat and pushing out your behind.

❷ Bring the kettlebell towards your left leg, and receive it in your left hand, which should come from behind the left leg.

❸ Repeat the movement with the left hand, giving the kettlebell from in front of the left leg to the right hand behind the right leg. This forms a figure 8 around your static legs.

TARGETS
- Abdominals
- Hamstrings
- Shoulders

BENEFITS
- Increases strength in the abdominals

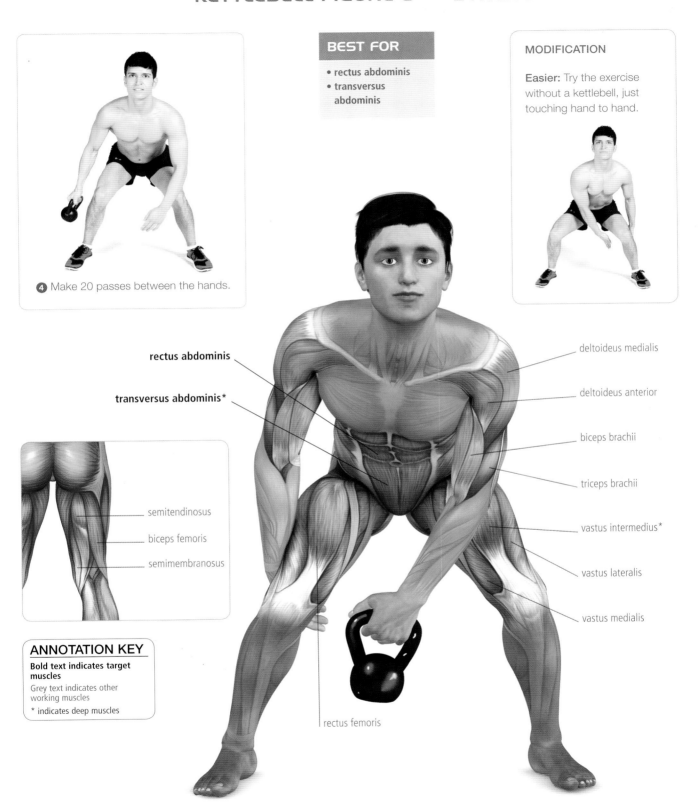

4 Make 20 passes between the hands.

BEST FOR

- rectus abdominis
- transversus abdominis

MODIFICATION

Easier: Try the exercise without a kettlebell, just touching hand to hand.

rectus abdominis

transversus abdominis*

deltoideus medialis

deltoideus anterior

biceps brachii

triceps brachii

vastus intermedius*

vastus lateralis

vastus medialis

semitendinosus

biceps femoris

semimembranosus

rectus femoris

ANNOTATION KEY

Bold text indicates target muscles

Grey text indicates other working muscles

* indicates deep muscles

BOTTOMS-UP KETTLEBELL CLEAN

TARGETS
• Forearms
• Biceps
• Shoulders

BENEFITS
• Increases strength in the forearms

① Stand upright, with your feet shoulder-width apart, holding a kettlebell in your left hand. Swing the kettlebell backwards, then bring it forwards and above your head forcefully, squeezing the handle as you do so.

DO IT RIGHT
• Keep your back straight throughout the movement.

AVOID
• Adopting a loose grip.

② Once your upper arm is parallel to the floor, hold the position, then lower your arm again. Complete 8–10 repetitions before switching to the other arm.

BEST FOR

- palmaris longus
- flexor carpi ulnaris
- pronator teres
- flexor digitorum
- anconeus
- extensor digitorum

extensor digitorum

anconeus

deltoideus anterior

deltoideus medialis

biceps brachii

triceps brachii

pectoralis minor*

pectoralis major

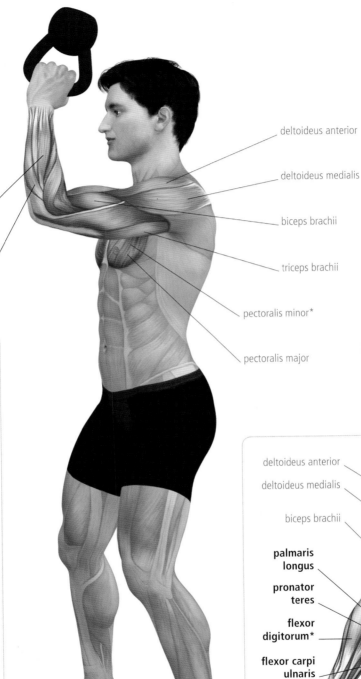

MODIFICATION

Easier: Try the exercise without a kettlebell.

ANNOTATION KEY

Bold text indicates target muscles

Grey text indicates other working muscles

* indicates deep muscles

deltoideus anterior

deltoideus medialis

biceps brachii

palmaris longus

pronator teres

flexor digitorum*

flexor carpi ulnaris

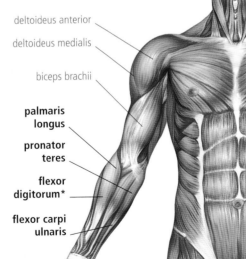

BAND PULL-APART

1 Stand with your feet shoulder-width apart, holding a band straight out in front of you. Your hands should also be shoulder-width apart.

DO IT RIGHT
• Keep your shoulders back.

AVOID
• Being carried by momentum.

TARGETS
• Shoulders
• Middle back
• Trapezius

BENEFITS
• Increases strength in the shoulders

2 Perform a fly motion, pulling the band across your chest and out to the sides, while keeping your palms facing down. Pause for a moment, then return to the starting position. Repeat 10–15 times.

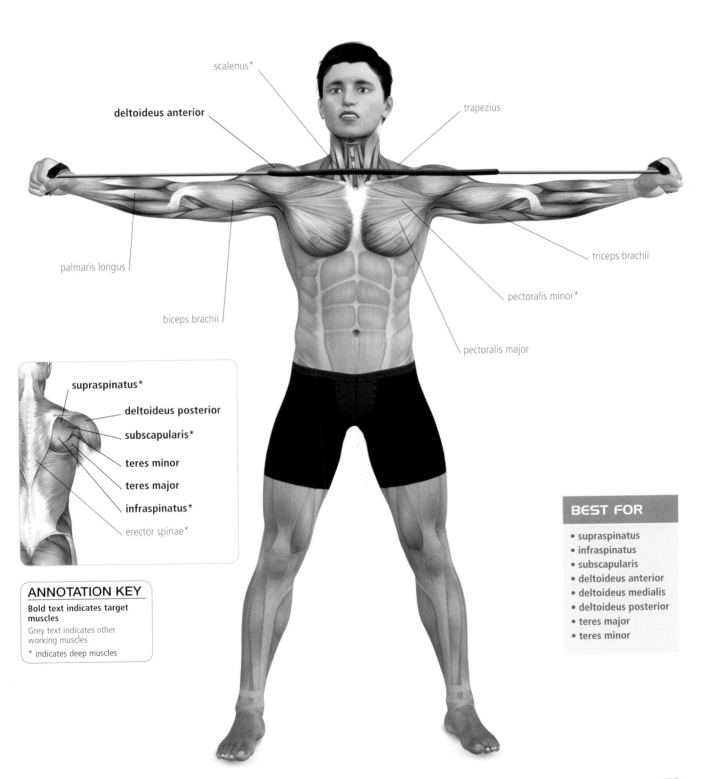

scalenus*

deltoideus anterior

trapezius

palmaris longus

triceps brachii

biceps brachii

pectoralis minor*

pectoralis major

supraspinatus*

deltoideus posterior

subscapularis*

teres minor

teres major

infraspinatus*

erector spinae*

ANNOTATION KEY

Bold text indicates target muscles

Grey text indicates other working muscles

* indicates deep muscles

BEST FOR

- supraspinatus
- infraspinatus
- subscapularis
- deltoideus anterior
- deltoideus medialis
- deltoideus posterior
- teres major
- teres minor

BAND GOOD MORNING (PULL-THROUGH)

❶ Loop a band around the base of a post. Step back a short distance and place the other end of the band over your head; it should sit on the back of your neck. Hold the band in place with your hands.

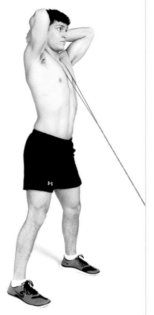

DO IT RIGHT
• Keep your back flat and your rear sticking out throughout the exercise.

AVOID
• Creating an excessive range of motion.

TARGETS
• Hamstrings
• Glutes
• Lower back

BENEFITS
• Increases power in the hamstrings

❷ Keeping your feet shoulder-width apart, your knees slightly bent and your back flat, lean forwards at the waist until your back is nearly parallel to the ground. Drive through the hips to return to the starting position. Complete 12–15 repetitions.

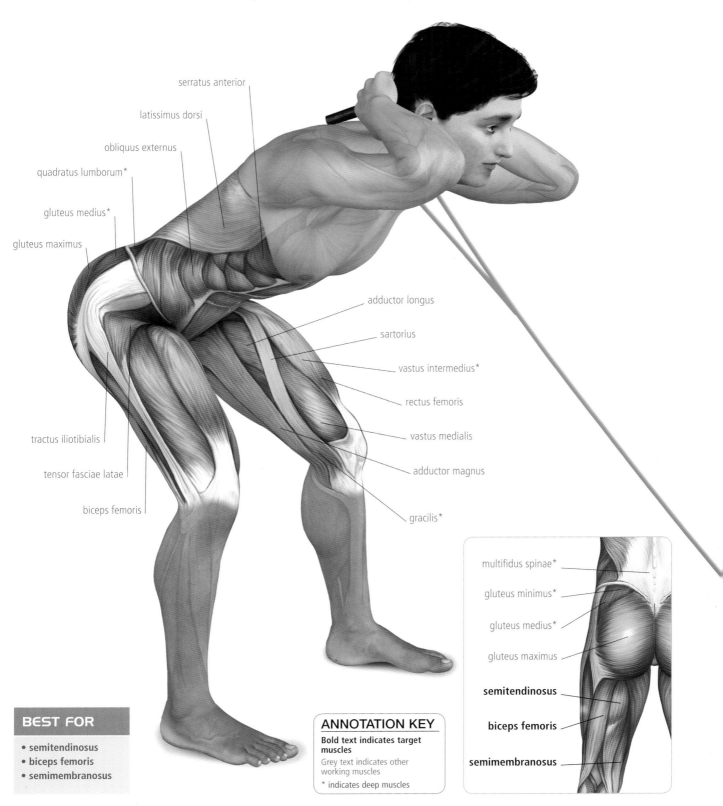

serratus anterior

latissimus dorsi

obliquus externus

quadratus lumborum*

gluteus medius*

gluteus maximus

tractus iliotibialis

tensor fasciae latae

biceps femoris

adductor longus

sartorius

vastus intermedius*

rectus femoris

vastus medialis

adductor magnus

gracilis*

multifidus spinae*

gluteus minimus*

gluteus medius*

gluteus maximus

semitendinosus

biceps femoris

semimembranosus

BEST FOR

- semitendinosus
- biceps femoris
- semimembranosus

ANNOTATION KEY

Bold text indicates target muscles

Grey text indicates other working muscles

* indicates deep muscles

EXTERNAL ROTATION WITH BAND

1 Fasten one end of a band around a post at elbow height. Grasp the other end with your right hand, keeping your upper arm pressed against your side and your forearm parallel to the ground.

TARGETS
• Shoulders

BENEFITS
• Builds strength in the shoulders

DO IT RIGHT
• Keep your upper arm against your side.

AVOID
• Working at an excessively fast pace.

2 Keeping your upper arm in position, move your forearm as far out to the side as you can before returning to the starting position. Complete 12–15 repetitions, then switch to the other arm.

BEST FOR

- supraspinatus
- infraspinatus
- deltoideus anterior
- deltoideus medialis
- deltoideus posterior
- teres major
- teres minor
- trapezius
- rhomboideus

ANNOTATION KEY

Bold text indicates target muscles

Grey text indicates other working muscles

* indicates deep muscles

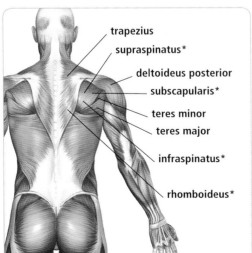

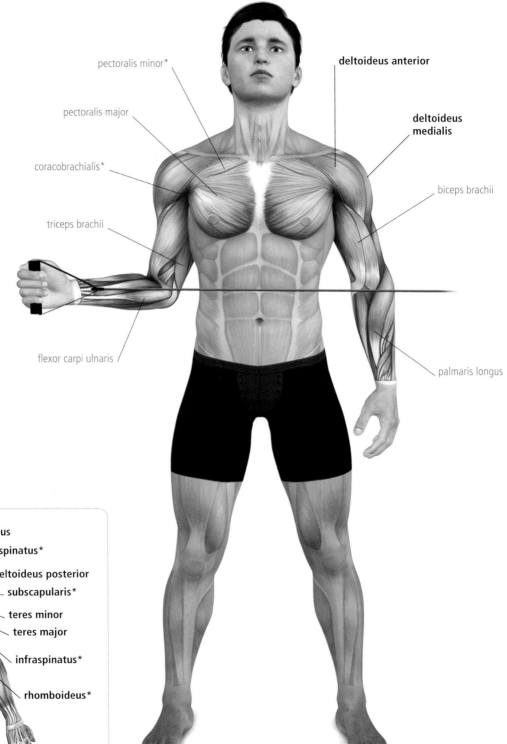

pectoralis minor*

pectoralis major

coracobrachialis*

triceps brachii

flexor carpi ulnaris

deltoideus anterior

deltoideus medialis

biceps brachii

palmaris longus

trapezius

supraspinatus*

deltoideus posterior

subscapularis*

teres minor

teres major

infraspinatus*

rhomboideus*

HIP EXTENSION WITH BAND

1 Loop one end of a band to the lower part of a post, and wrap the other end around your right ankle or foot.

2 Stand facing the post, holding a sturdy surface for support.

DO IT RIGHT
- Maintain an upright posture throughout the movement.

AVOID
- An excessive kicking motion.

TARGETS
- Glutes
- Hamstrings

BENEFITS
- Builds strength in the glutes

3 Maintaining an upright posture, extend the right leg as far back as you are able while also keeping it as straight as possible. Complete 10–12 repetitions, then switch legs.

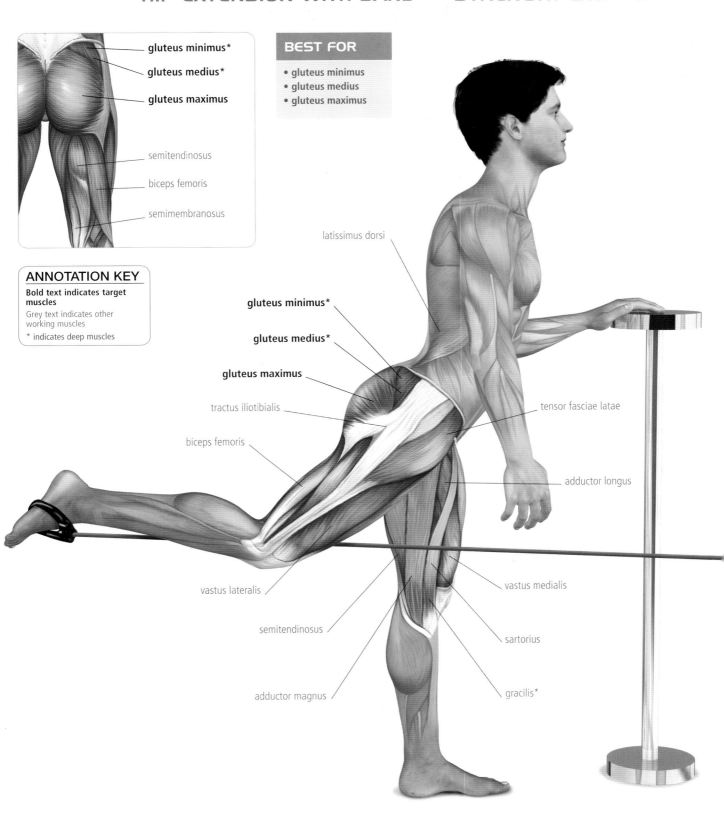

gluteus minimus*

gluteus medius*

gluteus maximus

semitendinosus

biceps femoris

semimembranosus

BEST FOR

- gluteus minimus
- gluteus medius
- gluteus maximus

ANNOTATION KEY

Bold text indicates target muscles

Grey text indicates other working muscles

* indicates deep muscles

latissimus dorsi

gluteus minimus*

gluteus medius*

gluteus maximus

tractus iliotibialis

biceps femoris

tensor fasciae latae

adductor longus

vastus lateralis

vastus medialis

semitendinosus

sartorius

adductor magnus

gracilis*

CONDITIONING EXERCISES

Conditioning training relies on aerobic activity – that is, repetitive, continuous movements often performed at an accelerated pace, working the heart.

In terms of methodologies, the scope is near limitless, since conditioning training utilises real-life movements – for example, an athlete moving quickly from linear to lateral positions over and over again. While speed is ill advised in strength training, it is recommended in conditioning, where the body itself is often the resistance, and the load placed on the muscles is low-impact.

Powered by adipose tissue, or fat, conditioning training will result in improved cardiovascular ability, endurance, stability and overall improved performance.

DEPTH JUMPS

1 Face two plyo boxes or platforms placed about a metre apart from each other, then stand on top of the one closest to you.

2 Jump off the plyo box; be sure to land between the two boxes on the balls of your feet.

TARGETS
- Quadriceps
- Hamstrings
- Glutes
- Calves

BENEFITS
- Improves speed, power and athleticism

MODIFICATIONS
- **Easier:** Use your arms to increase speed.
- **More difficult:** Use higher platforms.

DO IT RIGHT
- Be sure to maintain an erect posture throughout the movement.

AVOID
- Landing on your toes or heels.

3 As soon as your feet hit the ground, spring up on to the other box.

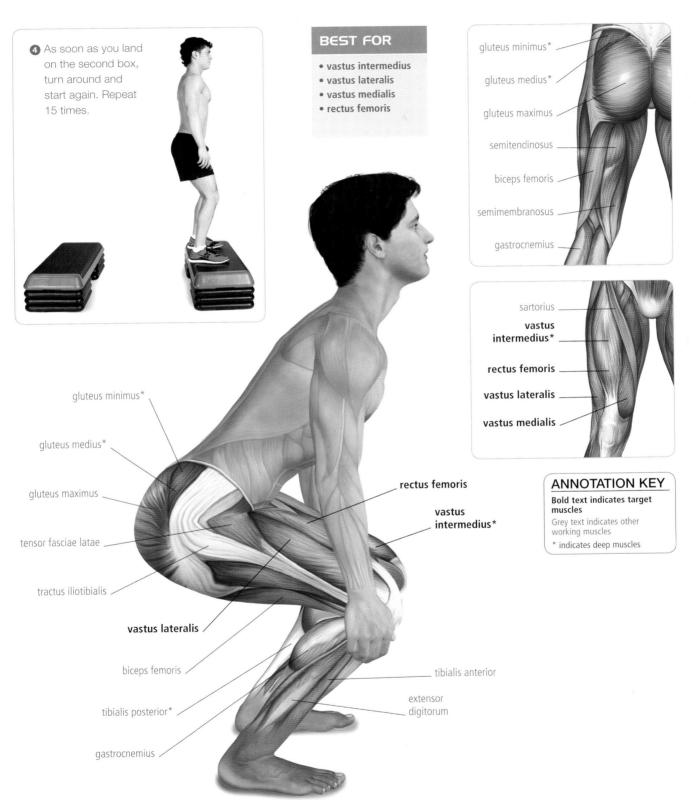

④ As soon as you land on the second box, turn around and start again. Repeat 15 times.

BEST FOR

- **vastus intermedius**
- **vastus lateralis**
- **vastus medialis**
- **rectus femoris**

gluteus minimus*

gluteus medius*

gluteus maximus

semitendinosus

biceps femoris

semimembranosus

gastrocnemius

sartorius

vastus intermedius*

rectus femoris

vastus lateralis

vastus medialis

ANNOTATION KEY

Bold text indicates target muscles

Grey text indicates other working muscles

* indicates deep muscles

gluteus minimus*

gluteus medius*

gluteus maximus

tensor fasciae latae

tractus iliotibialis

vastus lateralis

biceps femoris

tibialis posterior*

gastrocnemius

rectus femoris

vastus intermedius*

tibialis anterior

extensor digitorum

LATERAL BOUNDING

❶ Start in a quarter-squat position, then bound off your right foot as far and high as possible to your left.

❷ Be sure to land on your left foot.

TARGETS
- Quadriceps
- Hamstrings
- Glutes
- Calves

BENEFITS
- Helps you practise lateral movement at speed

MODIFICATIONS
- **Easier:** Try completing a set of jumps to one side, and then switch.
- **More difficult:** Perform the exercise while holding a medicine ball.

DO IT RIGHT
- Be sure to keep a tight core throughout the movement.

AVOID
- Allowing your knees to protrude past your toes.

❸ Next, bound as far and as high as possible back to your right off your left foot. Perform 15 repetitions per side.

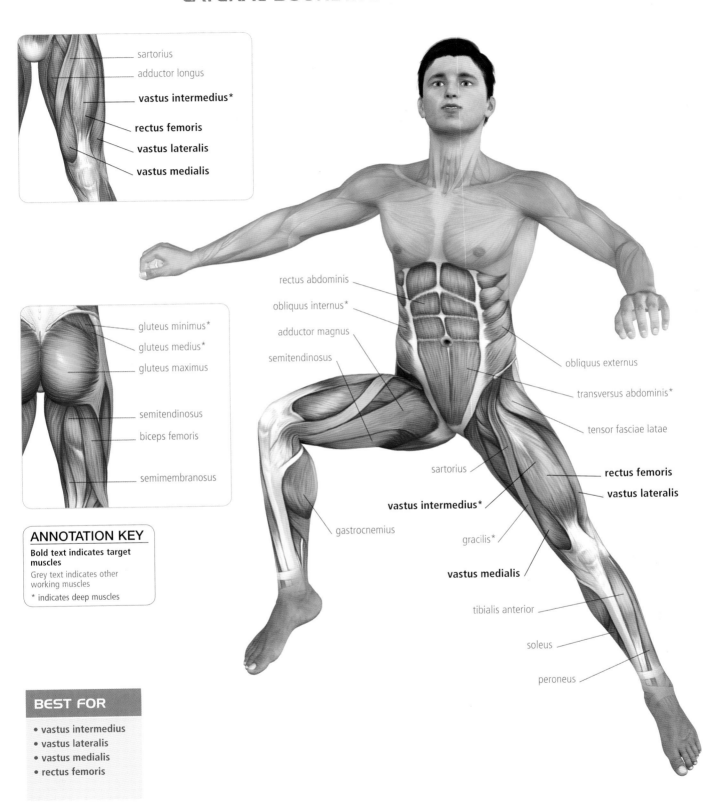

sartorius
adductor longus
vastus intermedius*
rectus femoris
vastus lateralis
vastus medialis

gluteus minimus*
gluteus medius*
gluteus maximus
semitendinosus
biceps femoris
semimembranosus

ANNOTATION KEY

Bold text indicates target muscles
Grey text indicates other working muscles
* indicates deep muscles

rectus abdominis
obliquus internus*
adductor magnus
semitendinosus
obliquus externus
transversus abdominis*
tensor fasciae latae
sartorius
rectus femoris
vastus lateralis
vastus intermedius*
gracilis*
gastrocnemius
vastus medialis
tibialis anterior
soleus
peroneus

BEST FOR

• vastus intermedius
• vastus lateralis
• vastus medialis
• rectus femoris

CONE JUMPS

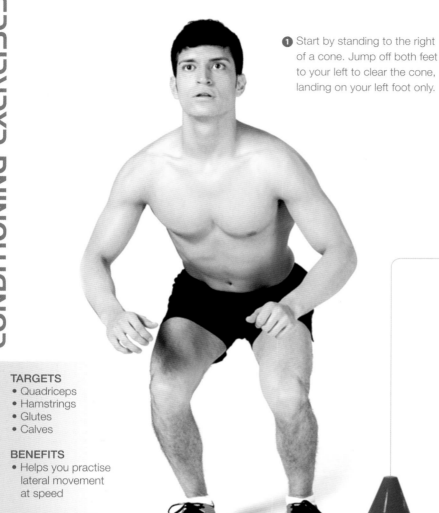

① Start by standing to the right of a cone. Jump off both feet to your left to clear the cone, landing on your left foot only.

DO IT RIGHT
- Be sure to keep a tight core throughout the movement.

AVOID
- Allowing your knees to protrude past your toes when landing.

TARGETS
- Quadriceps
- Hamstrings
- Glutes
- Calves

BENEFITS
- Helps you practise lateral movement at speed

MODIFICATIONS
- **Easier:** Complete a set of jumps to one side, and then switch.
- **More difficult:** Add a series of cones.

② Put your right foot down, and leap off both feet to clear the cone again. Be sure to land on your right foot this time. Only the foot that will be farthest away from the cone should make contact with the ground. Perform 15 repetitions per side.

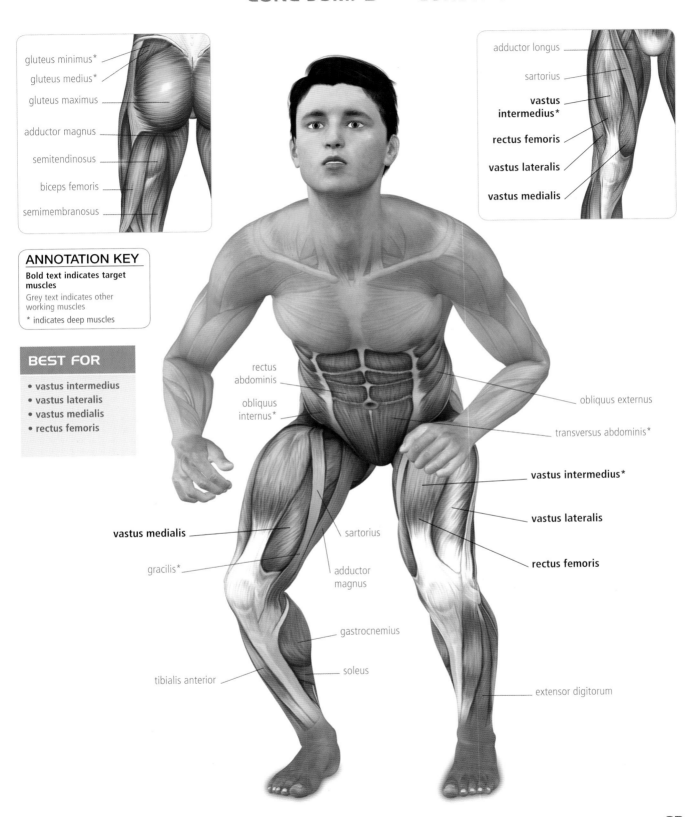

gluteus minimus*

gluteus medius*

gluteus maximus

adductor magnus

semitendinosus

biceps femoris

semimembranosus

adductor longus

sartorius

vastus intermedius*

rectus femoris

vastus lateralis

vastus medialis

ANNOTATION KEY

Bold text indicates target muscles

Grey text indicates other working muscles

* indicates deep muscles

BEST FOR

- **vastus intermedius**
- **vastus lateralis**
- **vastus medialis**
- **rectus femoris**

rectus abdominis

obliquus internus*

obliquus externus

transversus abdominis*

vastus intermedius*

vastus lateralis

rectus femoris

vastus medialis

gracilis*

sartorius

adductor magnus

gastrocnemius

tibialis anterior

soleus

extensor digitorum

BOX JUMPS

DO IT RIGHT
- Be sure to keep a tight core throughout the movement.

AVOID
- Landing excessively hard.

1 Start by standing in front of a plyo box or platform.

TARGETS
- Quadriceps
- Hamstrings
- Glutes
- Calves

BENEFITS
- Produces explosive power in your lower body

MODIFICATIONS
- **Easier:** Use a very low platform.
- **More difficult:** Use a higher platform.

2 Drop down into a quarter-squat in preparation for your jump.

3 Push through your heels, swing your arms and spring up on to the box.

BEST FOR

- vastus intermedius
- vastus lateralis
- vastus medialis
- rectus femoris

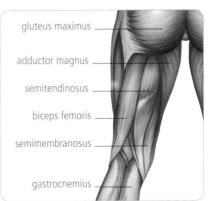

④ Land softly on your heels, then step down. Perform 15 repetitions.

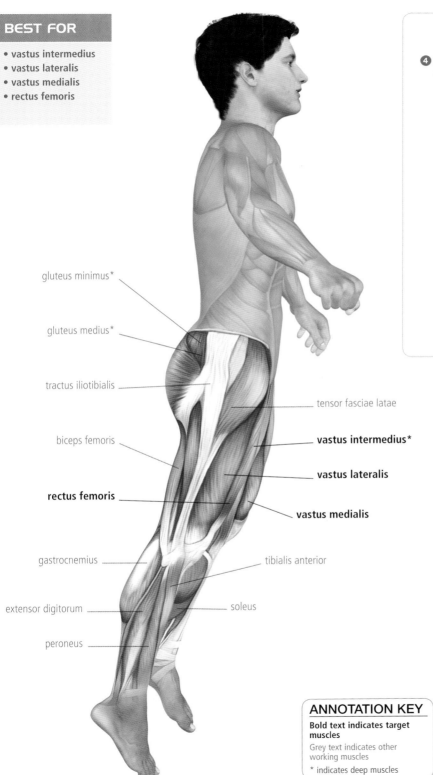

gluteus minimus*

gluteus medius*

tractus iliotibialis

biceps femoris

rectus femoris

gastrocnemius

extensor digitorum

peroneus

tensor fasciae latae

vastus intermedius*

vastus lateralis

vastus medialis

tibialis anterior

soleus

adductor longus

sartorius

vastus intermedius*

rectus femoris

vastus lateralis

vastus medialis

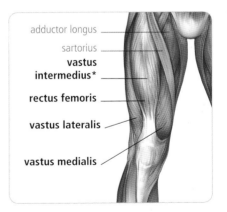

gluteus maximus

adductor magnus

semitendinosus

biceps femoris

semimembranosus

gastrocnemius

ANNOTATION KEY

Bold text indicates target muscles

Grey text indicates other working muscles

* indicates deep muscles

BURPEES

1 Start in a squat position, with your hands firmly planted on the floor, shoulder-width apart.

DO IT RIGHT
- Be sure to keep a tight core throughout the movement.

AVOID
- Landing excessively hard.

TARGETS
- Glutes
- Quadriceps
- Hamstrings
- Erectors
- Calves

BENEFITS
- Increases both muscular strength and endurance

MODIFICATIONS
- **Easier:** Jump at a very low height.
- **More difficult:** Add a push-up to the routine.

2 Kick your feet back and straighten your legs into a push-up position.

3 Quickly return to the squat position.

4 Leap vertically from the squat position as high as possible, raising your arms as you jump. Complete 15 repetitions.

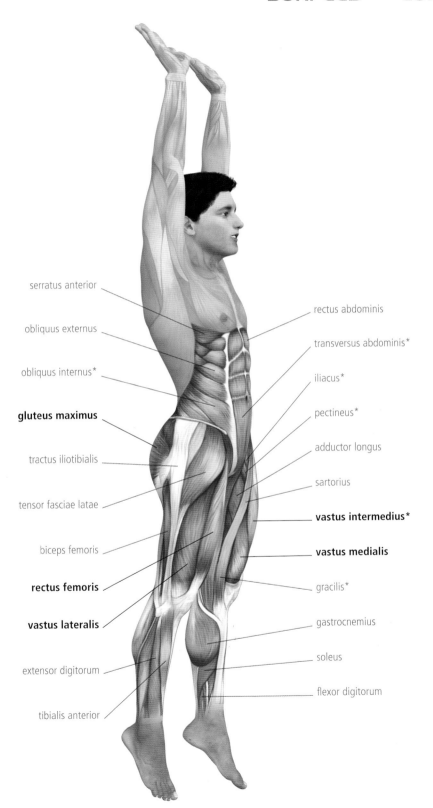

ANNOTATION KEY

Bold text indicates target muscles

Grey text indicates other working muscles

* indicates deep muscles

serratus anterior

obliquus externus

obliquus internus*

gluteus maximus

tractus iliotibialis

tensor fasciae latae

biceps femoris

rectus femoris

vastus lateralis

extensor digitorum

tibialis anterior

rectus abdominis

transversus abdominis*

iliacus*

pectineus*

adductor longus

sartorius

vastus intermedius*

vastus medialis

gracilis*

gastrocnemius

soleus

flexor digitorum

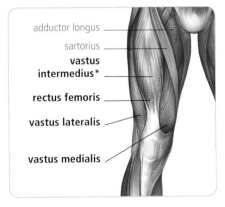

adductor longus

sartorius

vastus intermedius*

rectus femoris

vastus lateralis

vastus medialis

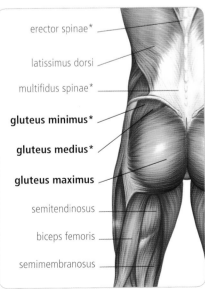

erector spinae*

latissimus dorsi

multifidus spinae*

gluteus minimus*

gluteus medius*

gluteus maximus

semitendinosus

biceps femoris

semimembranosus

AIR SQUATS

1 Stand tall, with your feet shoulder-width apart, your toes pointed slightly outwards and your arms extended in front of you.

DO IT RIGHT
- Squat deep, and be sure to keep your thighs parallel to the floor.

AVOID
- Hyperextending your knees past your toes while squatting.

2 Inhale as you bend your knees, while keeping your back flat. Lower yourself towards the floor until your thighs are parallel to it.

TARGETS
- Quadriceps
- Hamstrings
- Glutes
- Core

BENEFITS
- Increases power and mass in the thighs

MODIFICATIONS
- **Easier:** Place a Swiss ball against a wall and lean your lower back into it.
- **More difficult:** Bringing your feet closer together increases the effort required.

3 Exhale as you push through your heels to stand erect. Perform 12–15 repetitions.

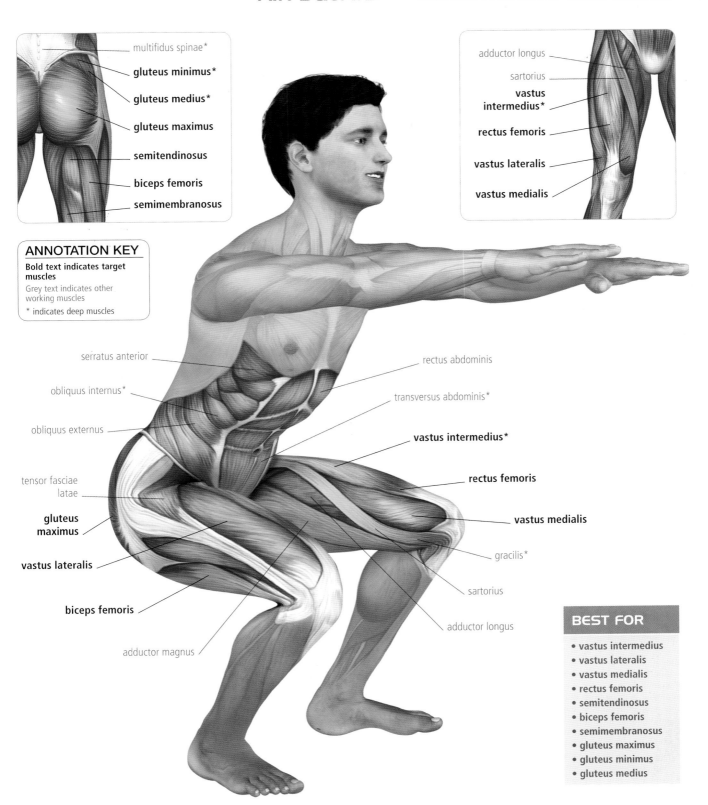

multifidus spinae*

gluteus minimus*

gluteus medius*

gluteus maximus

semitendinosus

biceps femoris

semimembranosus

adductor longus

sartorius

vastus intermedius*

rectus femoris

vastus lateralis

vastus medialis

ANNOTATION KEY

Bold text indicates target muscles

Grey text indicates other working muscles

* indicates deep muscles

serratus anterior

obliquus internus*

obliquus externus

tensor fasciae latae

gluteus maximus

vastus lateralis

biceps femoris

adductor magnus

rectus abdominis

transversus abdominis*

vastus intermedius*

rectus femoris

vastus medialis

gracilis*

sartorius

adductor longus

BEST FOR

- vastus intermedius
- vastus lateralis
- vastus medialis
- rectus femoris
- semitendinosus
- biceps femoris
- semimembranosus
- gluteus maximus
- gluteus minimus
- gluteus medius

CROSSOVER STEP-UP

① Stand to the right of a bench.

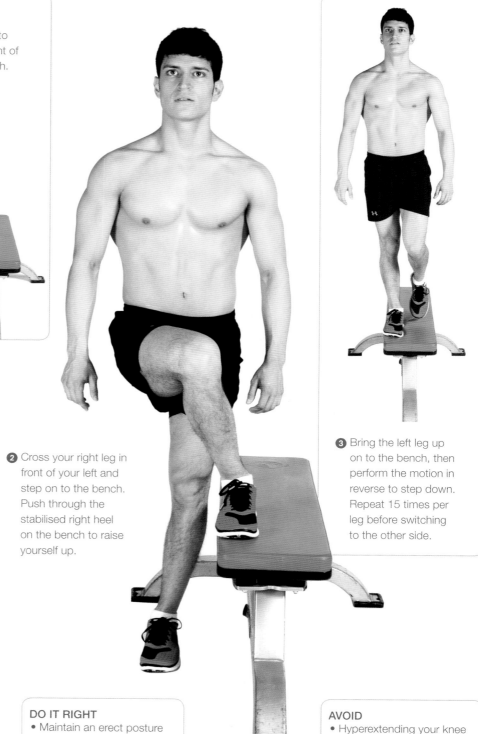

② Cross your right leg in front of your left and step on to the bench. Push through the stabilised right heel on the bench to raise yourself up.

③ Bring the left leg up on to the bench, then perform the motion in reverse to step down. Repeat 15 times per leg before switching to the other side.

TARGETS
- Quadriceps
- Hamstrings
- Glutes
- Core

BENEFITS
- Increases power and explosiveness in the thighs

MODIFICATIONS
- **Easier:** Try holding a stick or broom for support.
- **More difficult:** Hold a pair of dumbbells for increased resistance.

DO IT RIGHT
- Maintain an erect posture throughout the movement.

AVOID
- Hyperextending your knee past your toes.

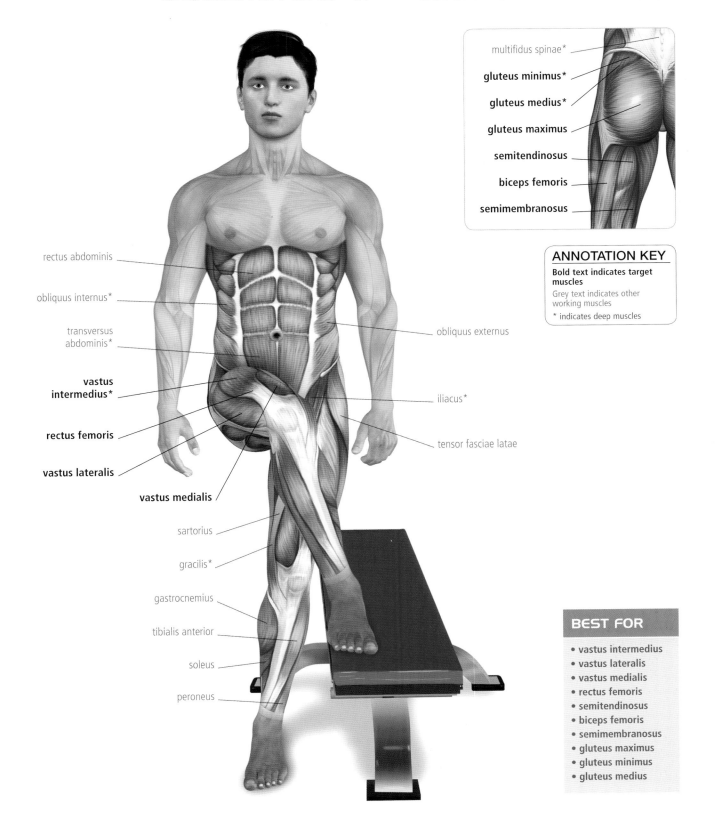

multifidus spinae*
gluteus minimus*
gluteus medius*
gluteus maximus
semitendinosus
biceps femoris
semimembranosus

ANNOTATION KEY

Bold text indicates target muscles
Grey text indicates other working muscles
* indicates deep muscles

rectus abdominis

obliquus internus*

transversus
abdominis*

**vastus
intermedius***

rectus femoris

vastus lateralis

vastus medialis

sartorius

gracilis*

gastrocnemius

tibialis anterior

soleus

peroneus

obliquus externus

iliacus*

tensor fasciae latae

BEST FOR

- vastus intermedius
- vastus lateralis
- vastus medialis
- rectus femoris
- semitendinosus
- biceps femoris
- semimembranosus
- gluteus maximus
- gluteus minimus
- gluteus medius

REVERSE LUNGE

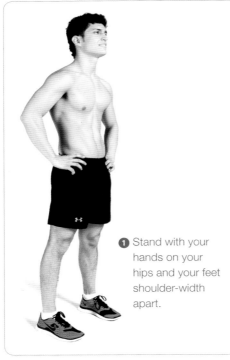

1 Stand with your hands on your hips and your feet shoulder-width apart.

2 Take a big step backwards, bending your knees as you do so.

TARGETS
- Quadriceps
- Glutes
- Hamstrings

BENEFITS
- Strengthens the quadriceps and glutes

DO IT RIGHT
- Maintain an erect posture throughout the movement.

AVOID
- Hyperextending your knee past your toes when lunging.

3 When the front thigh is roughly parallel to the ground, push through your front heel to return to the starting position. Perform 15 repetitions per leg.

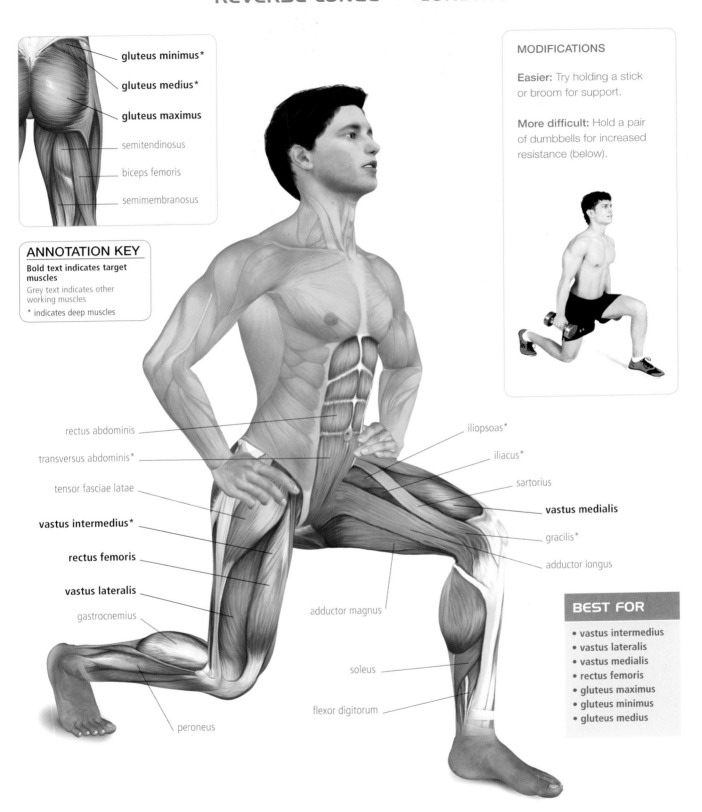

gluteus minimus*

gluteus medius*

gluteus maximus

semitendinosus

biceps femoris

semimembranosus

ANNOTATION KEY

Bold text indicates target muscles

Grey text indicates other working muscles

* indicates deep muscles

MODIFICATIONS

Easier: Try holding a stick or broom for support.

More difficult: Hold a pair of dumbbells for increased resistance (below).

rectus abdominis

transversus abdominis*

tensor fasciae latae

vastus intermedius*

rectus femoris

vastus lateralis

gastrocnemius

peroneus

adductor magnus

soleus

flexor digitorum

iliopsoas*

iliacus*

sartorius

vastus medialis

gracilis*

adductor longus

BEST FOR

- vastus intermedius
- vastus lateralis
- vastus medialis
- rectus femoris
- gluteus maximus
- gluteus minimus
- gluteus medius

MOUNTAIN CLIMBERS

1 Begin in a completed push-up position, with your body in a straight line.

2 Bend one leg and bring your knee as close to your chest as you are able.

TARGETS
- Quadriceps
- Glutes
- Hamstrings
- Calves
- Core

BENEFITS
- Increases cardiovascular ability and power in the legs

MODIFICATION
- **More difficult:** Wear ankle weights for increased resistance.

3 Return to the starting position, and repeat with the other leg.

DO IT RIGHT
- Keep your back flat throughout the movement.

AVOID
- Excessively swinging your hips throughout the motion.

4 Perform this exercise for up to 2 minutes.

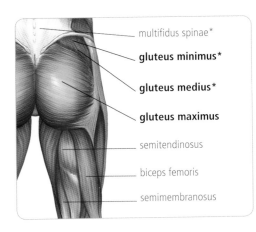

- multifidus spinae*
- **gluteus minimus***
- **gluteus medius***
- **gluteus maximus**
- semitendinosus
- biceps femoris
- semimembranosus

ANNOTATION KEY
Bold text indicates target muscles
Grey text indicates other working muscles
* indicates deep muscles

BEST FOR
- **vastus intermedius**
- **vastus lateralis**
- **vastus medialis**
- **rectus femoris**
- **gluteus maximus**
- **gluteus minimus**
- **gluteus medius**

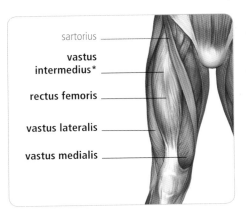

- sartorius
- **vastus intermedius***
- **rectus femoris**
- **vastus lateralis**
- **vastus medialis**

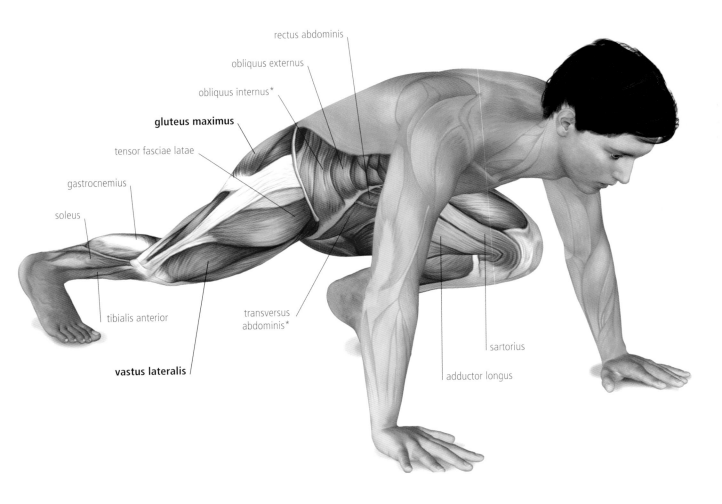

- rectus abdominis
- obliquus externus
- obliquus internus*
- **gluteus maximus**
- tensor fasciae latae
- gastrocnemius
- soleus
- tibialis anterior
- **vastus lateralis**
- transversus abdominis*
- sartorius
- adductor longus

STAR JUMPS

1 Start by crouching down in a half-squat position, with your arms slightly bent in front of you and your hands crossed over each other.

TARGETS
- Quadriceps
- Hamstrings
- Glutes
- Calves

BENEFITS
- Produces explosive power in your lower body

MODIFICATIONS
- **Easier:** Jump at a very low height.
- **More difficult:** Add a higher jump.

DO IT RIGHT
- Be sure to keep a tight core throughout the movement.

AVOID
- Landing excessively hard.

2 Push off your heels and leap straight up, extending your legs to the side and raising your arms as you do so. Land softly on your heels, and return to the starting position. Perform 15 repetitions.

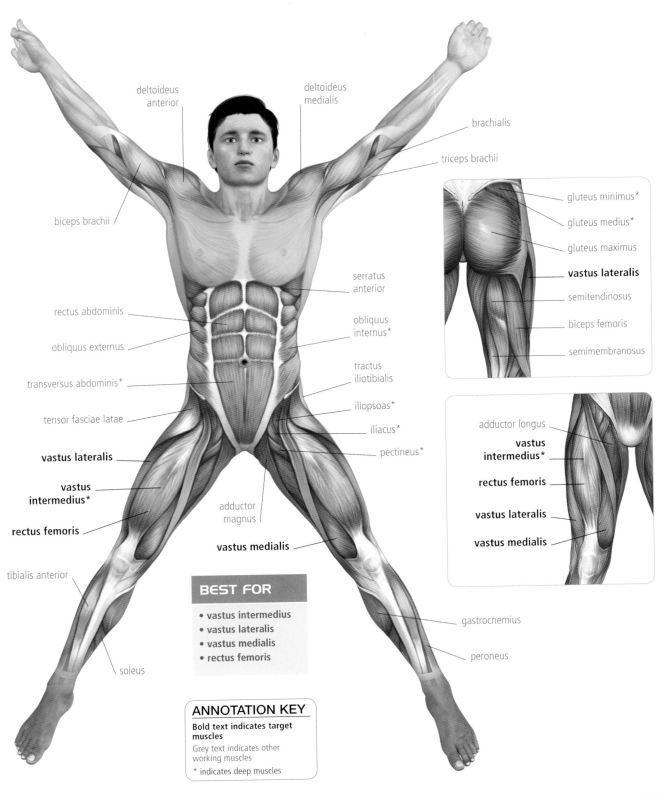

deltoideus anterior

deltoideus medialis

brachialis

triceps brachii

biceps brachii

gluteus minimus*

gluteus medius*

gluteus maximus

vastus lateralis

semitendinosus

biceps femoris

semimembranosus

serratus anterior

rectus abdominis

obliquus internus*

obliquus externus

tractus iliotibialis

transversus abdominis*

iliopsoas*

iliacus*

tensor fasciae latae

pectineus*

adductor longus

vastus intermedius*

vastus lateralis

rectus femoris

vastus lateralis

vastus medialis

vastus intermedius*

rectus femoris

adductor magnus

vastus medialis

tibialis anterior

BEST FOR

- vastus intermedius
- vastus lateralis
- vastus medialis
- rectus femoris

gastrocnemius

peroneus

soleus

ANNOTATION KEY

Bold text indicates target muscles

Grey text indicates other working muscles

* indicates deep muscles

PLYOMETRIC PUSH-UP

1 Start in a standard push-up position.

2 Lower yourself until your upper arms are parallel to the floor, then prepare to return to the starting position.

TARGETS
- Pectorals
- Deltoids
- Triceps
- Upper back
- Core

BENEFITS
- Produces explosive power in the upper body

MODIFICATIONS
- **Easier:** Try it without clapping.
- **More difficult:** Add resistance weights on your wrists.

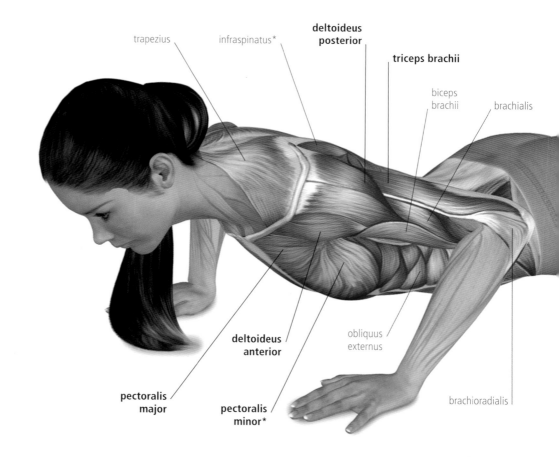

trapezius

infraspinatus*

deltoideus posterior

triceps brachii

biceps brachii

brachialis

deltoideus anterior

obliquus externus

pectoralis major

pectoralis minor*

brachioradialis

DO IT RIGHT
• Keep a tight core throughout the movement.

AVOID
• Putting excessive strain on your wrists.

3 As you push up, quickly clap your hands together before safely touching them back to the floor. Perform 15 repetitions.

deltoideus medialis

deltoideus anterior

pectoralis minor*

pectoralis major

serratus anterior

rectus abdominis

obliquus externus

obliquus internus*

transversus abdominis*

BEST FOR

• pectoralis major
• pectoralis minor
• deltoideus anterior
• deltoideus posterior
• deltoideus medialis
• triceps brachii

ANNOTATION KEY

Bold text indicates target muscles
Grey text indicates other working muscles
* indicates deep muscles

SKIER

CONDITIONING EXERCISES

1 Begin in a push-up position, with your legs resting on a Swiss ball.

DO IT RIGHT
• Keep a tight core throughout the movement.

AVOID
• Excessive speed.

TARGETS
• Hips
• Core
• Upper back
• Posterior deltoids

BENEFITS
• Increases great stability in the hips and core

MODIFICATION
• **Easier:** Try rotating to one side only.

2 While maintaining your core position, rotate your trunk quickly to the left so that your legs are stacked on top of each other.

3 Return to the starting position, and perform the same movement to the right. Complete 15 full rotations.

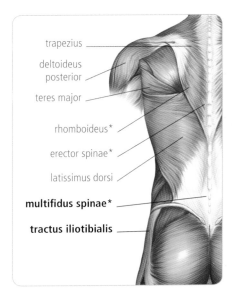

trapezius

deltoideus posterior

teres major

rhomboideus*

erector spinae*

latissimus dorsi

multifidus spinae*

tractus iliotibialis

ANNOTATION KEY

Bold text indicates target muscles

Grey text indicates other working muscles

* indicates deep muscles

BEST FOR

- sartorius
- iliopsoas
- iliacus
- tensor fasciae latae
- tractus iliotibialis
- rectus abdominis
- transversus abdominis
- multifidus spinae
- obliquus externus
- obliquus internus

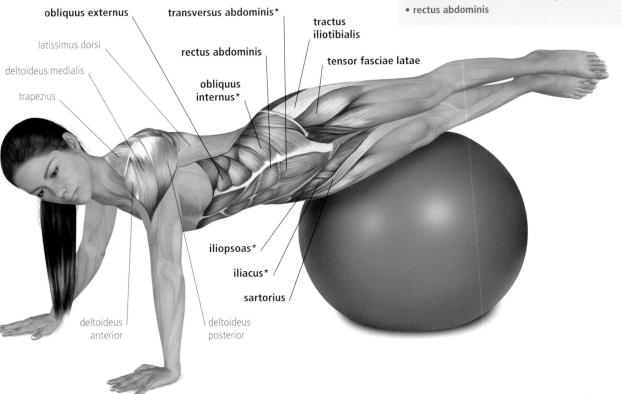

obliquus externus

transversus abdominis*

tractus iliotibialis

latissimus dorsi

rectus abdominis

tensor fasciae latae

deltoideus medialis

obliquus internus*

trapezius

iliopsoas*

iliacus*

sartorius

deltoideus anterior

deltoideus posterior

TURKISH GET-UP

1 Lie flat on your back. Your right arm should be raised straight out above your chest, and your left arm should be at your side.

2 Flex your right knee and place your right foot flat on the floor.

DO IT RIGHT
- Keep a tight core throughout the movement.

AVOID
- Performing the exercise at excessive speed.

TARGETS
- Shoulders
- Core
- Thighs
- Glutes
- Upper back
- Triceps

BENEFITS
- Increases stability in the hips and aids balance throughout the body

MODIFICATION
- **More difficult:** Perform the exercise with a dumbbell or kettlebell overhead.

3 Rotate your core slightly to the left and lift your shoulders off the floor, supporting your weight on your left forearm. Next, plant your left hand on the floor and lift yourself up to a sitting position.

4 Lift your hips skywards and tuck your left leg under your body to support yourself on your left knee.

5 Lift your left hand off the floor and push through your right foot to a standing position, keeping your right arm stretched over your head throughout the exercise.

6 Return to the starting position. Perform 10 repetitions per arm.

ANNOTATION KEY

Bold text indicates target muscles

Grey text indicates other working muscles

* indicates deep muscles

BEST FOR

- **deltoideus anterior**
- **deltoideus posterior**
- **deltoideus medialis**
- **rectus abdominis**
- **transversus abdominis**
- **obliquus externus**
- **obliquus internus**
- **multifidus spinae**
- **vastus intermedius**
- **vastus lateralis**
- **vastus medialis**
- **rectus femoris**
- **semitendinosus**
- **biceps femoris**
- **semimembranosus**
- **gluteus minimus**
- **gluteus medius**
- **gluteus maximus**

deltoideus posterior
trapezius
rhomboideus*
erector spinae*
multifidus spinae*
gluteus minimus*
gluteus medius*
gluteus maximus
semitendinosus
biceps femoris
semimembranosus

biceps brachii
deltoideus anterior
triceps brachii
deltoideus medialis
vastus medialis
sartorius
rectus abdominis
transversus abdominis*
brachialis
obliquus externus
obliquus internus*
biceps femoris
vastus lateralis
rectus femoris
vastus intermedius*
tensor fasciae latae

FARMER'S WALK

DO IT RIGHT
- Keep a tight core throughout the movement.

AVOID
- Holding excessive weights.

1 Begin in a standing position, feet shoulder-width apart, holding a pair of kettlebells or dumbbells by your side.

TARGETS
- Rectus abdominis
- Erector spinae
- Forearms
- Biceps

BENEFITS
- Helps develop grip strength in your forearms, as well as core stability

MODIFICATIONS
- **Easier:** Carry a lighter load.
- **More difficult:** Carry a heavier load.

2 Walk rapidly a pre-determined distance or time (for example, the length of the gym or 20 seconds) with the resistance. Lower the weights, rest and repeat 3 times.

BEST FOR

- rectus abdominis
- erector spinae

ANNOTATION KEY

Bold text indicates target muscles

Grey text indicates other working muscles

* indicates deep muscles

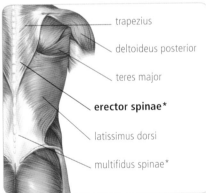

trapezius

deltoideus posterior

teres major

erector spinae*

latissimus dorsi

multifidus spinae*

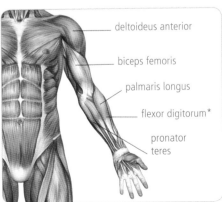

deltoideus anterior

biceps femoris

palmaris longus

flexor digitorum*

pronator teres

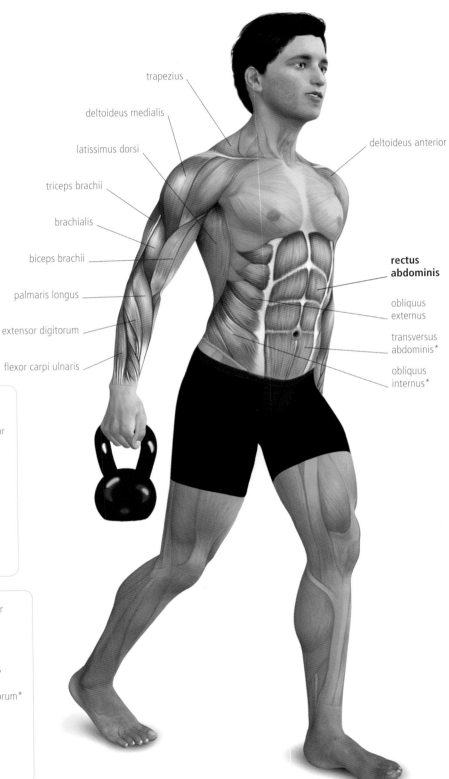

trapezius

deltoideus medialis

latissimus dorsi

triceps brachii

brachialis

biceps brachii

palmaris longus

extensor digitorum

flexor carpi ulnaris

deltoideus anterior

rectus abdominis

obliquus externus

transversus abdominis*

obliquus internus*

PULLOVER PASS

❶ Lying on your back, with your knees bent and your feet flat on the floor, hold a medicine ball behind your head at arms' length.

TARGETS
- Rectus abdominis
- Erector spinae

BENEFITS
- Develops explosive strength in the abdominals

DO IT RIGHT
- Keep a tight core throughout the movement.

AVOID
- Putting too much stress on your neck.

❷ Quickly sit up, and pass the ball to a partner while contracting your abdominals.

❸ Receive the ball back, and gently return to the starting position. Complete 25 repetitions.

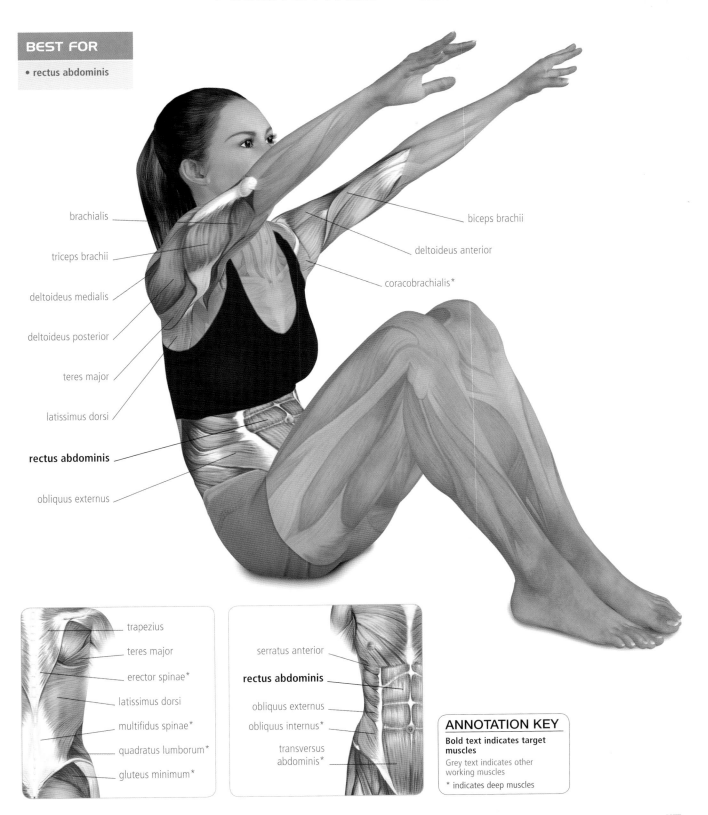

BEST FOR

• rectus abdominis

brachialis

triceps brachii

deltoideus medialis

deltoideus posterior

teres major

latissimus dorsi

rectus abdominis

obliquus externus

biceps brachii

deltoideus anterior

coracobrachialis*

trapezius

teres major

erector spinae*

latissimus dorsi

multifidus spinae*

quadratus lumborum*

gluteus minimum*

serratus anterior

rectus abdominis

obliquus externus

obliquus internus*

transversus abdominis*

ANNOTATION KEY

Bold text indicates target muscles

Grey text indicates other working muscles

* indicates deep muscles

MEDICINE BALL PIKE-UP

① Begin in a standard push-up position, with your hands shoulder-width apart and your toes planted on a medicine ball.

DO IT RIGHT
• Keep your legs locked throughout the movement.

AVOID
• Lowering your torso further than parallel to the floor.

TARGETS
• Core
• Glutes
• Hamstrings
• Calves

BENEFITS
• Builds strength and stability in the core

② Raise your hips to the ceiling, rolling the medicine ball towards your hands as you do so.

③ Reverse the movement, lowering yourself back down to the starting position. Complete 15 repetitions.

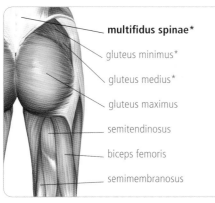

multifidus spinae*
gluteus minimus*
gluteus medius*
gluteus maximus
semitendinosus
biceps femoris
semimembranosus

MODIFICATIONS

Easier: Perform the exercise without a medicine ball (right).

More difficult: Raise one leg off the medicine ball.

ANNOTATION KEY

Bold text indicates target muscles

Grey text indicates other working muscles

* indicates deep muscles

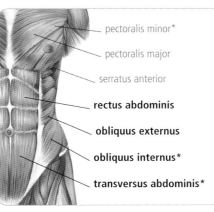

pectoralis minor*
pectoralis major
serratus anterior
rectus abdominis
obliquus externus
obliquus internus*
transversus abdominis*

gluteus maximus
tractus iliotibialis
quadratus lumborum*
multifidus spinae*
obliquus internus*
latissimus dorsi

vastus lateralis
biceps femoris
gastrocnemius
extensor digitorum
rectus femoris
tibialis anterior
peroneus
tensor fasciae latae
rectus abdominis
obliquus externus

BEST FOR

- rectus abdominis
- transversus abdominis
- obliquus externus
- obliquus internus
- multifidus spinae

PLANK

① Position yourself on all fours.

TARGETS
- Rectus abdominis
- Erector spinae
- Obliques

BENEFITS
- Strengthens the entire core

MODIFICATION
- **More difficult:** Lift one foot off the floor for a greater challenge.

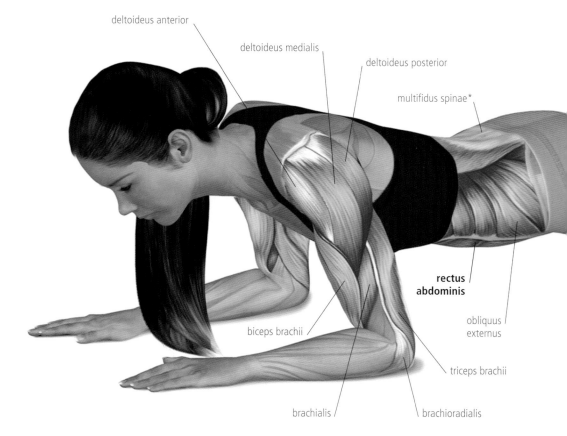

deltoideus anterior

deltoideus medialis

deltoideus posterior

multifidus spinae*

rectus abdominis

obliquus externus

biceps brachii

triceps brachii

brachialis

brachioradialis

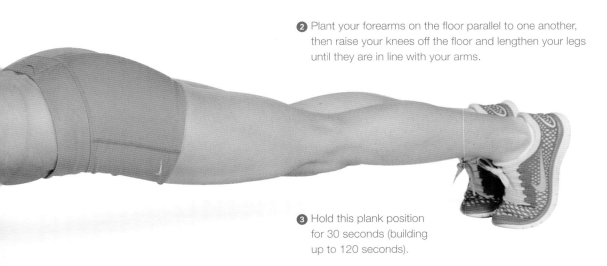

2 Plant your forearms on the floor parallel to one another, then raise your knees off the floor and lengthen your legs until they are in line with your arms.

3 Hold this plank position for 30 seconds (building up to 120 seconds).

DO IT RIGHT
- Keep your abdominal muscles tight and your body in a straight line.

AVOID
- Bridging too high, since this can take stress off working muscles.

ANNOTATION KEY
Bold text indicates target muscles
Grey text indicates other working muscles
* indicates deep muscles

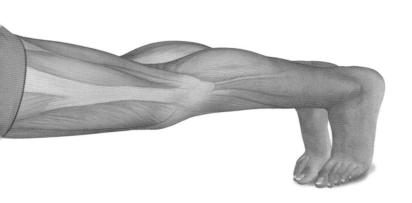

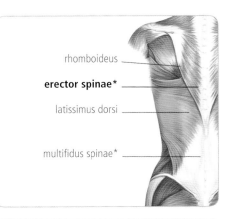

rhomboideus

erector spinae*

latissimus dorsi

multifidus spinae*

BEST FOR
- **rectus abdominis**
- **erector spinae**

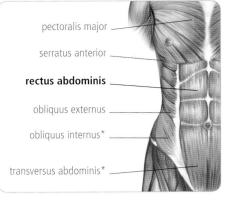

pectoralis major

serratus anterior

rectus abdominis

obliquus externus

obliquus internus*

transversus abdominis*

SIDE PLANK

① Lie on your right side with your legs extended, one on top of the other. Your right arm should be bent at a 90-degree angle, with your fingers facing forwards. Rest your left arm along your left hip.

TARGETS
- Lower abdominals
- Erector spinae
- Deltoids

BENEFITS
- Strengthens the abdominals, lower back and shoulders

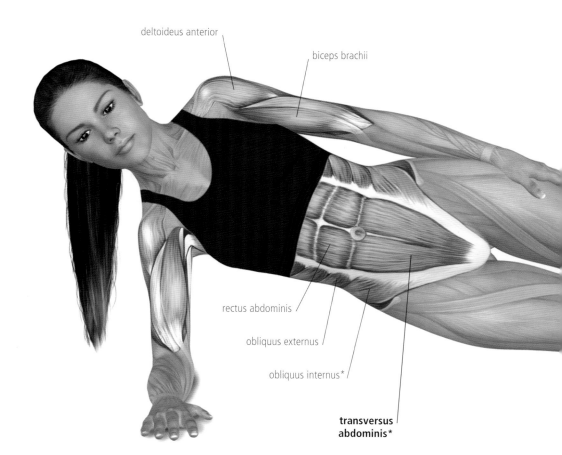

deltoideus anterior

biceps brachii

rectus abdominis

obliquus externus

obliquus internus*

transversus abdominis*

MODIFICATIONS

Easier: Use your resting arm as an anchor, assisting with the lift.

More difficult: Open your legs slightly while in hold (right).

❷ Pushing through your right forearm, raise your hips off the ground until your body is one straight line. Hold this position for 30 seconds (working up to 1 full minute), then switch to your left side and repeat.

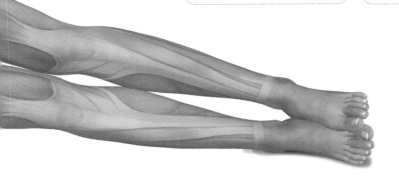

BEST FOR

- **transversus abdominis**
- **erector spinae**

DO IT RIGHT
- Push evenly from both your forearm and hips.

AVOID
- Placing too much strain on your shoulders.

ANNOTATION KEY

Bold text indicates target muscles

Grey text indicates other working muscles

* indicates deep muscles

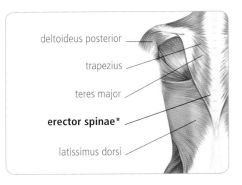

deltoideus posterior

trapezius

teres major

erector spinae*

latissimus dorsi

T-STABILISATION

DO IT RIGHT
• Keep your body in one straight line.

AVOID
• Arching or bridging your back.

❶ Start in the finished push-up position, with your arms extended to full lockout and your palms facing forwards, supporting yourself on your toes.

TARGETS
• Abdominals
• Hips
• Lower back
• Obliques

BENEFITS
• Strengthens the abdominals, hips, lower back and obliques

❷ While keeping your body in one straight line, turn your left hip skywards, allowing your left foot to rest on the right. Raise your right arm laterally across your body until it points to the ceiling. Hold this position for 30 seconds (working up to 60 seconds). Return to the starting position, and repeat with the other side.

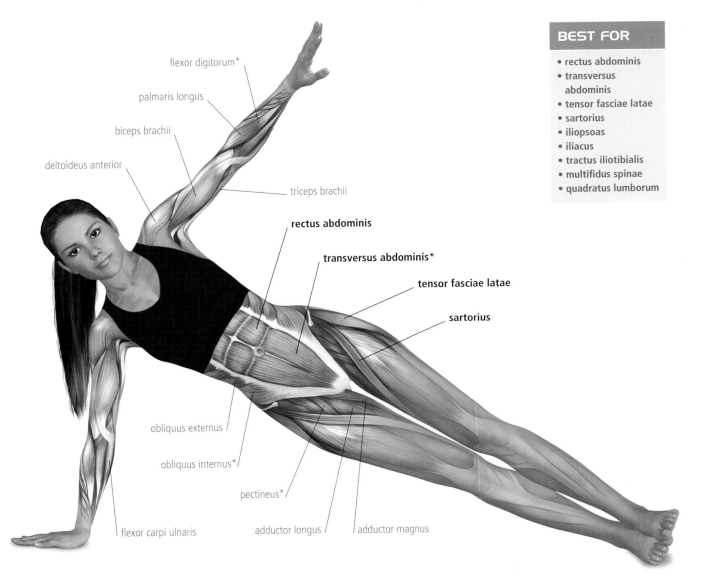

flexor digitorum*

palmaris longus

biceps brachii

deltoideus anterior

triceps brachii

rectus abdominis

transversus abdominis*

tensor fasciae latae

sartorius

obliquus externus

obliquus internus*

pectineus*

flexor carpi ulnaris

adductor longus

adductor magnus

BEST FOR

- rectus abdominis
- transversus abdominis
- tensor fasciae latae
- sartorius
- iliopsoas
- iliacus
- tractus iliotibialis
- multifidus spinae
- quadratus lumborum

ANNOTATION KEY

Bold text indicates target muscles

Grey text indicates other working muscles

* indicates deep muscles

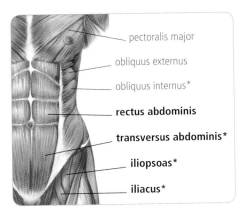

pectoralis major

obliquus externus

obliquus internus*

rectus abdominis

transversus abdominis*

iliopsoas*

iliacus*

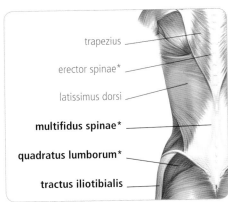

trapezius

erector spinae*

latissimus dorsi

multifidus spinae*

quadratus lumborum*

tractus iliotibialis

SWISS BALL ROLL-OUT

❶ Kneel in front of a Swiss ball, and place your hands on it at about hip height.

❷ Slowly roll the ball forwards, extending your body as you go.

❸ Keep rolling forwards until you are completely stretched out while keeping a flat back and remaining anchored on your knees. Then, using your abdominals and lower-back muscles, roll back to the starting position. Perform 15–20 repetitions.

TARGETS
- Abdominals
- Lower back
- Obliques

BENEFITS
- Helps stabilise the core

MODIFICATION
- **Easier:** Plant your feet against a solid surface for extra support.

DO IT RIGHT
- Keep your body elongated throughout the movement.

BEST FOR

- rectus abdominis
- transversus abdominis
- multifidus spinae
- quadratus lumborum

latissimus dorsi

obliquus externus

obliquus internus*

gluteus maximus

tensor fasciae latae

biceps femoris

rectus abdominis

transversus abdominis*

sartorius

vastus intermedius*

rectus femoris

vastus medialis

vastus lateralis

ANNOTATION KEY

Bold text indicates target muscles

Grey text indicates other working muscles

* indicates deep muscles

AVOID
- Bridging your back and allowing your hips to sag.

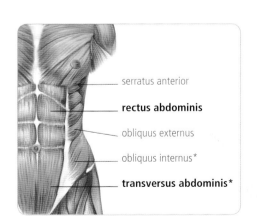

serratus anterior

rectus abdominis

obliquus externus

obliquus internus*

transversus abdominis*

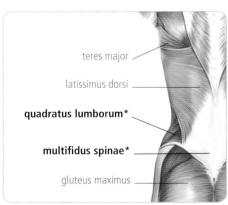

teres major

latissimus dorsi

quadratus lumborum*

multifidus spinae*

gluteus maximus

SWISS BALL JACKKNIFE

❶ Start on all fours, with your hands shoulder-width apart. Raise your left leg and place it on top of the Swiss ball, then do the same with your right leg, so that you are in a push-up position with your shins resting on the Swiss ball.

DO IT RIGHT
• Brace your core.

AVOID
• Rounding your back.

TARGETS
• Hip flexors
• Rectus abdominis
• Erectors
• Obliques

BENEFITS
• Strengthens your hip flexors, as well as your rectus abdominis and erectors

MODIFICATION
• **More difficult:** Try taking one leg off the ball for added resistance.

❷ Bend your knees, rolling the ball in towards your chest as far as you are able, then extend your legs back out to the starting position. Complete 20 repetitions.

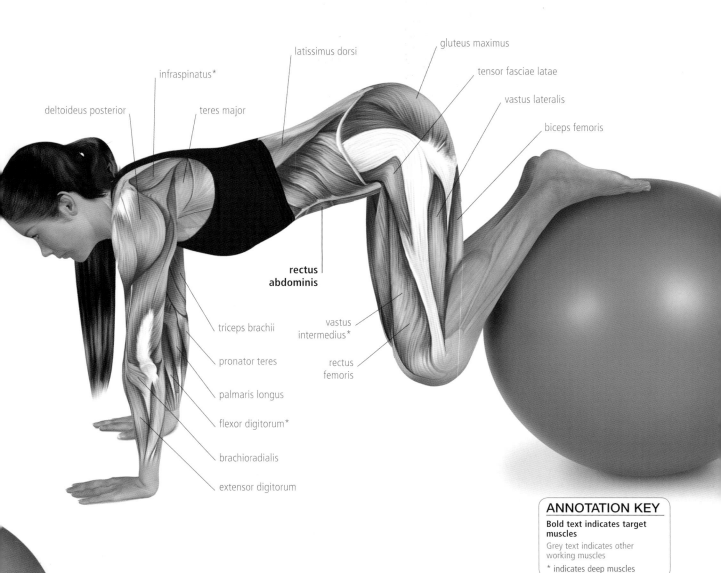

infraspinatus*

latissimus dorsi

gluteus maximus

tensor fasciae latae

vastus lateralis

biceps femoris

deltoideus posterior

teres major

rectus abdominis

triceps brachii

vastus intermedius*

rectus femoris

pronator teres

palmaris longus

flexor digitorum*

brachioradialis

extensor digitorum

ANNOTATION KEY

Bold text indicates target muscles

Grey text indicates other working muscles

* indicates deep muscles

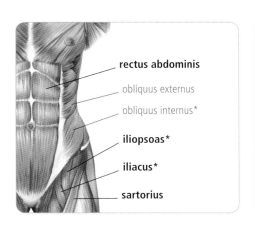

rectus abdominis

obliquus externus

obliquus internus*

iliopsoas*

iliacus*

sartorius

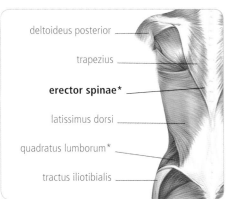

deltoideus posterior

trapezius

erector spinae*

latissimus dorsi

quadratus lumborum*

tractus iliotibialis

BEST FOR

- sartorius
- iliopsoas
- iliacus
- rectus abdominis
- erector spinae

BENT-KNEE SIT-UP

① Lie on your back with your legs bent so that your feet are tucked as close to your buttocks as possible. Either put your hands on your head or cross your arms over your chest.

TARGETS
- Hip flexors
- Rectus abdominis
- Erectors
- Obliques

BENEFITS
- Strengthens your hip flexors, rectus abdominis and erectors

MODIFICATION
- **More difficult:** Execute the exercise with one leg raised off the floor.

② Flex your trunk towards your thighs until your back is off the floor, then lower yourself back down. Repeat 25 times.

BENT-KNEE SIT-UP • CONDITIONING EXERCISES

DO IT RIGHT
• Be sure to engage your core, not your neck.

AVOID
• Rounding your back.

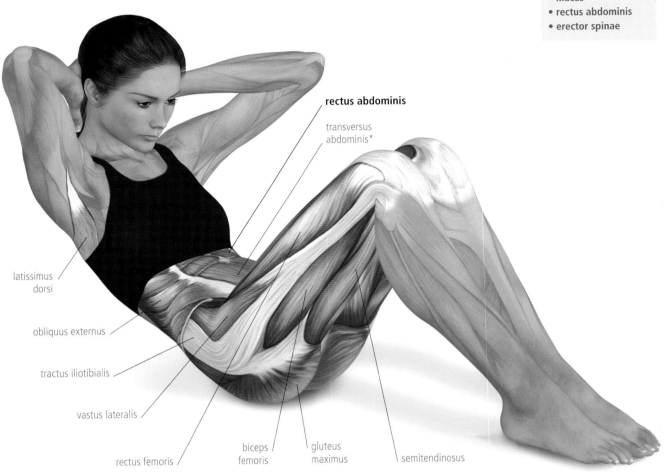

rectus abdominis

transversus abdominis*

latissimus dorsi

obliquus externus

tractus iliotibialis

vastus lateralis

rectus femoris

biceps femoris

gluteus maximus

semitendinosus

ANNOTATION KEY

Bold text indicates target muscles

Grey text indicates other working muscles

* indicates deep muscles

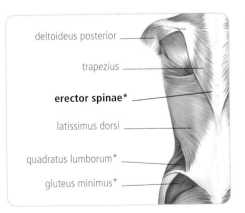

deltoideus posterior

trapezius

erector spinae*

latissimus dorsi

quadratus lumborum*

gluteus minimus*

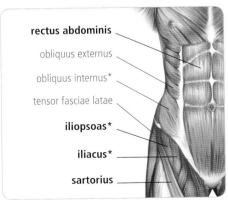

rectus abdominis

obliquus externus

obliquus internus*

tensor fasciae latae

iliopsoas*

iliacus*

sartorius

STABILITY BALL EXCHANGE

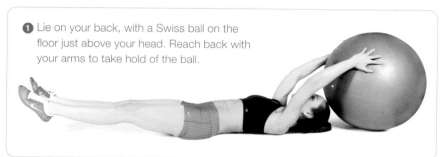

1 Lie on your back, with a Swiss ball on the floor just above your head. Reach back with your arms to take hold of the ball.

DO IT RIGHT
- Complete a full range of motion.

AVOID
- Kicking up with your legs.

2 With the ball in hand, raise both your upper body and your thighs, moving them towards each other.

TARGETS
- Hip flexors
- Rectus abdominis
- Erectors

BENEFITS
- Strengthens the hip flexors and rectus abdominis

MODIFICATION
- **More difficult:** Try using a medicine ball instead of a Swiss ball.

3 Place the Swiss ball between your legs, then lower all your limbs back to the floor, bringing your arms beside your head.

4 Repeat the movement, this time passing the Swiss ball from your legs to your hands. Complete 15 exchanges.

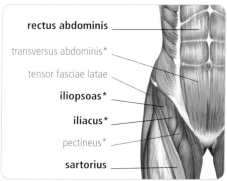

rectus abdominis
transversus abdominis*
tensor fasciae latae
iliopsoas*
iliacus*
pectineus*
sartorius

ANNOTATION KEY
Bold text indicates target muscles
Grey text indicates other working muscles
* indicates deep muscles

BEST FOR
- sartorius
- iliopsoas
- iliacus
- rectus abdominis

deltoideus posterior
trapezius
erector spinae*
latissimus dorsi
quadratus lumborum*
gluteus minimus*

rectus abdominis

vastus medialis
vastus lateralis
rectus femoris
vastus intermedius*
biceps femoris
tensor fasciae latae
tractus iliotibialis
gluteus maximus

trapezius
teres major
obliquus externus
obliquus internus*

MEDICINE BALL WOOD-CHOP

DO IT RIGHT
• Perform the positive portion of the exercise (swinging) aggressively and the negative portion (the wind-up) in a slow, controlled fashion, all the while keeping your core contracted and tight.

AVOID
• Twisting too violently from side to side, since this can throw your back out.

TARGETS
• Obliques
• Rectus abdominis
• Erectors

BENEFITS
• Strengthen the obliques

❶ Stand upright, with your feet shoulder-width apart, holding a medicine ball with both hands to the right side of your head.

❷ Twist your core towards the left while lowering the medicine ball to the outside of your left leg, then return to the starting position. Repeat 20 times, then switch to the other side.

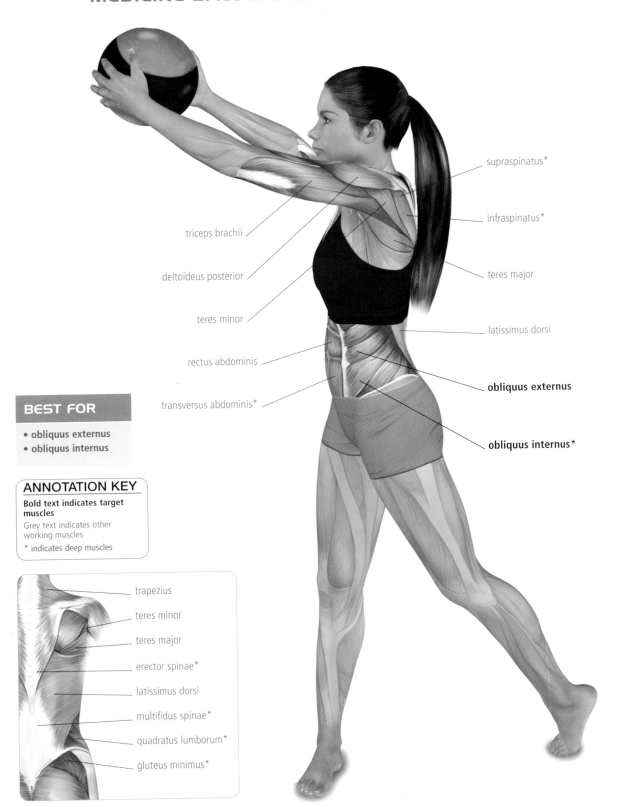

supraspinatus*

infraspinatus*

teres major

triceps brachii

latissimus dorsi

deltoideus posterior

obliquus externus

teres minor

rectus abdominis

obliquus internus*

transversus abdominis*

BEST FOR

- **obliquus externus**
- **obliquus internus**

ANNOTATION KEY

Bold text indicates target muscles
Grey text indicates other working muscles
* indicates deep muscles

trapezius

teres minor

teres major

erector spinae*

latissimus dorsi

multifidus spinae*

quadratus lumborum*

gluteus minimus*

MEDICINE BALL SLAM

DO IT RIGHT
• Keep your torso straight on throughout the movement.

AVOID
• Rounding your back excessively.

❶ Stand upright with your feet shoulder-width apart and knees slightly bent, holding a medicine ball above your head with arms outstretched.

TARGETS
• Rectus abdominis
• Deltoids
• Upper back

BENEFITS
• Is effective for engaging and readying the frontal core

❷ Keeping your back straight, lean forwards at the waist and forcefully throw the ball on to the floor. Pick up the ball and repeat 20 times.

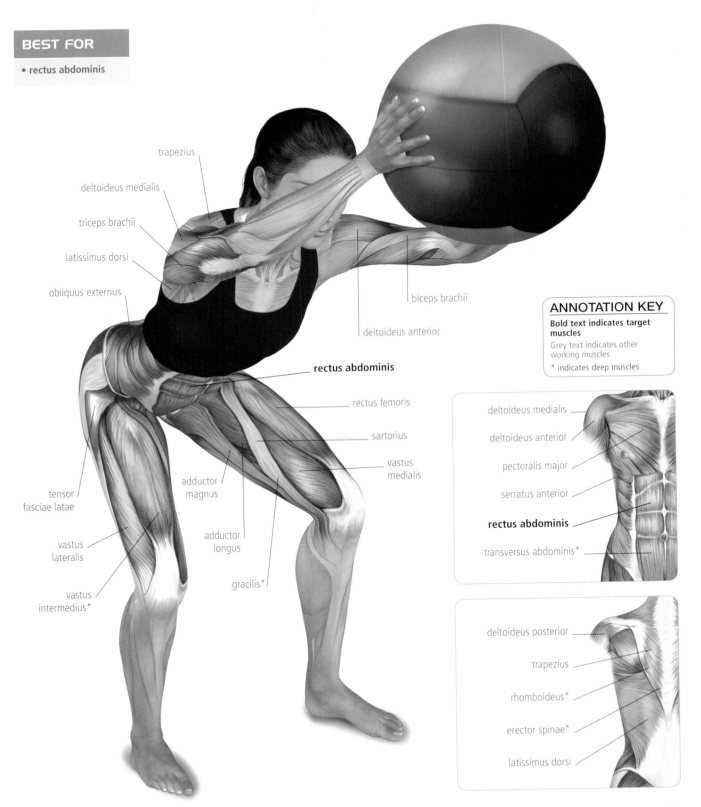

BEST FOR

• rectus abdominis

trapezius

deltoideus medialis

triceps brachii

latissimus dorsi

obliquus externus

biceps brachii

deltoideus anterior

ANNOTATION KEY

Bold text indicates target muscles

Grey text indicates other working muscles

* indicates deep muscles

rectus abdominis

rectus femoris

sartorius

vastus medialis

tensor fasciae latae

adductor magnus

vastus lateralis

adductor longus

vastus intermedius*

gracilis*

deltoideus medialis

deltoideus anterior

pectoralis major

serratus anterior

rectus abdominis

transversus abdominis*

deltoideus posterior

trapezius

rhomboideus*

erector spinae*

latissimus dorsi

SEATED RUSSIAN TWIST

1 Sit on the floor with your legs bent, knees slightly apart, holding a Swiss ball in front of you at arms' length. Lean back slightly to activate the core, keeping a flat back.

TARGETS
- Rectus abdominis
- Obliques
- Erector spinae

BENEFITS
- Strengthens the major muscles of the core

DO IT RIGHT
- Twist in a controlled motion and not too fast.

AVOID
- Rounding your back.

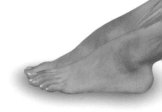

2 Rotate your torso to the left as far as you can comfortably go.

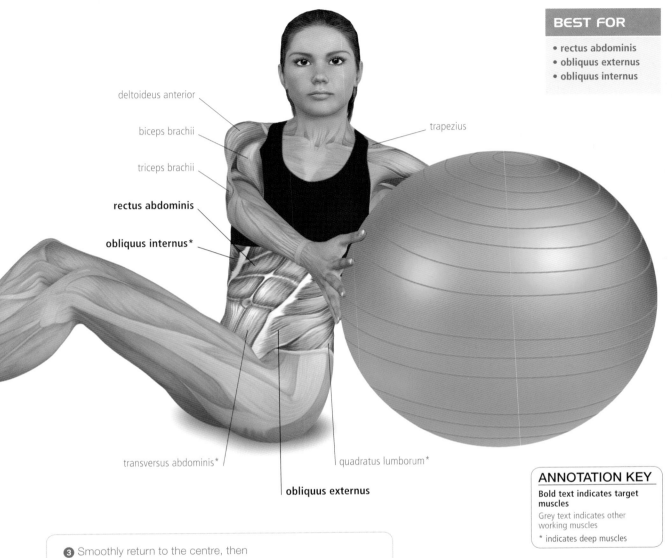

BEST FOR

- rectus abdominis
- obliquus externus
- obliquus internus

deltoideus anterior

biceps brachii

triceps brachii

rectus abdominis

obliquus internus*

trapezius

transversus abdominis*

quadratus lumborum*

obliquus externus

ANNOTATION KEY

Bold text indicates target muscles

Grey text indicates other working muscles

* indicates deep muscles

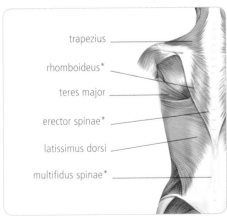

❸ Smoothly return to the centre, then continue the rotation as far to the right as possible, before returning to the centre again. This is one rotation; complete 20 full rotations.

trapezius

rhomboideus*

teres major

erector spinae*

latissimus dorsi

multifidus spinae*

SWISS BALL HIP CROSSOVER

1 Lie on your back with your arms stretched out to your sides. Place your legs on a Swiss ball, with your glutes close to it, bending your knees at 90 degrees.

TARGETS
- Lower back
- Obliques
- Rectus abdominis

BENEFITS
- Strengthens the lower back and obliques

MODIFICATION
- **More difficult:** Try holding a medicine ball between your thighs for added resistance.

DO IT RIGHT
- Keep your core centred.

AVOID
- Swinging your legs excessively.

2 Brace your abdominals, and lower your legs to the right side until they are as close to the floor as possible. Do not lift your shoulders off the floor.

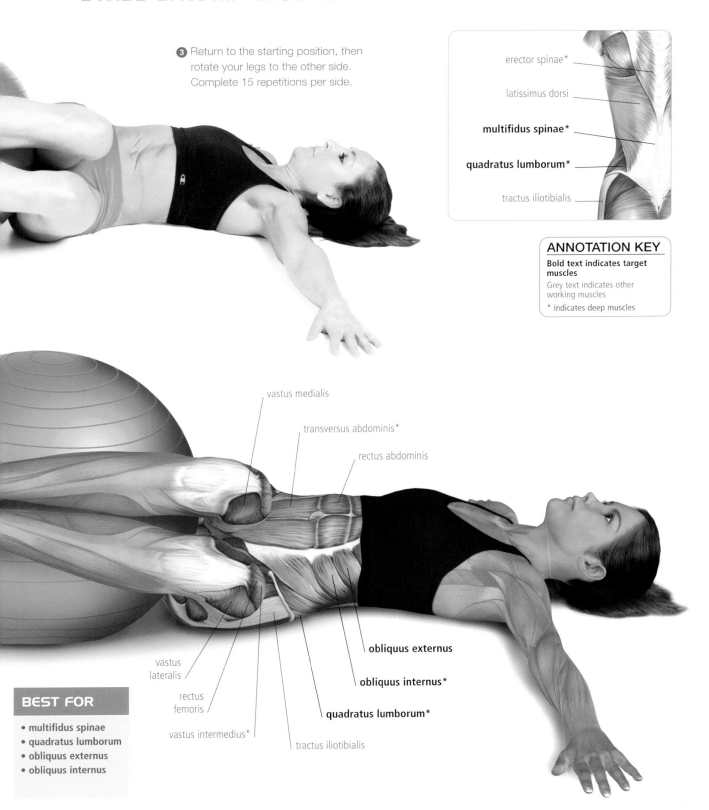

3 Return to the starting position, then rotate your legs to the other side. Complete 15 repetitions per side.

erector spinae*

latissimus dorsi

multifidus spinae*

quadratus lumborum*

tractus iliotibialis

ANNOTATION KEY

Bold text indicates target muscles

Grey text indicates other working muscles

* indicates deep muscles

vastus medialis

transversus abdominis*

rectus abdominis

obliquus externus

obliquus internus*

quadratus lumborum*

vastus lateralis

rectus femoris

vastus intermedius*

tractus iliotibialis

BEST FOR

• multifidus spinae
• quadratus lumborum
• obliquus externus
• obliquus internus

KNEELING CABLE CRUNCH

1 Begin on your knees in front of a weight stack, facing away from it. Set the weight to a moderate resistance, and attach a looped rope to its cable.

2 Hold the rope loosely around your neck using both hands.

DO IT RIGHT
• Keep your core engaged throughout the movement.

AVOID
• Swinging your back excessively.

TARGETS
• Rectus abdominis
• Obliques
• Erector spinae

BENEFITS
• Strengthens your abdominal muscles

MODIFICATION
• **More difficult:** Try crunching side to side for added resistance.

3 Bend forward at the waist, keeping your neck tucked in, and crunch downward, until your elbows are resting on your thighs. Contract the abs and return to the starting position. Perform 30 repetitions.

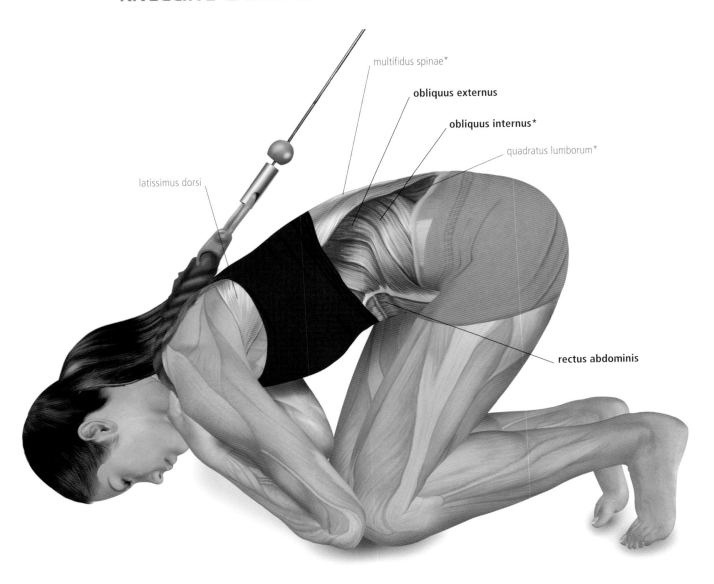

multifidus spinae*

obliquus externus

obliquus internus*

quadratus lumborum*

latissimus dorsi

rectus abdominis

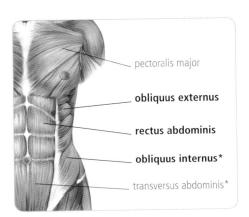

pectoralis major

obliquus externus

rectus abdominis

obliquus internus*

transversus abdominis*

BEST FOR

- **rectus abdominis**
- **obliquus externus**
- **obliquus internus**

ANNOTATION KEY

Bold text indicates target muscles

Grey text indicates other working muscles

* indicates deep muscles

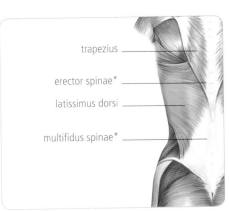

trapezius

erector spinae*

latissimus dorsi

multifidus spinae*

WORKOUTS

The following theme-based workouts will help you make the most of your strength and conditioning training. Always commit yourself fully to a given exercise rather than rush through it. You should also allow enough time to make each movement as effective as possible. Challenge yourself further by executing each movement to the best of your ability instead of attempting to complete a sequence more quickly. Enjoy!

BEGINNER'S WORKOUT

As its name suggests, this workout is suitable for everybody, especially those new to strength and conditioning training.

① Barbell Squats, page 28

② Barbell Deadlift, page 32

③ Bench Press, page 34

④ Standing Barbell Press, page 40

⑤ Dips, page 48

6 Depth Jumps, page 88

7 Reverse Lunge, page 102

8 Pullover Pass, page 116

9 Plank, page 120

10 Swiss Ball Roll-Out, page 126

147

SPORTS WORKOUT

The focus here is on flexibility for improved sporting performance.

1 Alternating Renegade Row, page 64

2 Advanced Kettlebell Windmill, page 72

3 Kettlebell Figure 8, page 74

4 Lateral Bounding, page 90

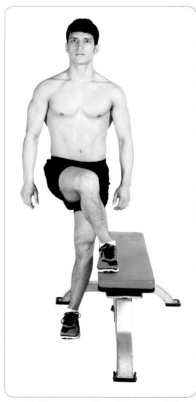

5 Crossover Step-Up, page 100

6 Skier, page 110

7 T-Stabilisation, page 124

8 Medicine Ball Wood-Chop, page 134

9 Seated Russian Twist, page 138

10 Swiss Ball Hip Crossover, page 140

MIXED-MODALITIES WORKOUT

The emphasis of this workout is on using various pieces of equipment for both strength and conditioning training.

1 Barbell Squat Snatch, page 30

2 Dumbbell Pullover, page 46

3 Reverse Close-Grip Front Chin, page 52

4 Alternating Kettlebell Press, page 66

5 Plyo Kettlebell Push-Up, page 70

⑥ Band Pull-Apart, page 78

⑦ Box Jumps, page 94

⑧ Turkish Get-Up, page 112

⑨ Swiss Ball Jackknife, page 128

⑩ Medicine Ball Slam, page 136

RANGE WORKOUT

This sequence of exercises is designed to improve your flexibility, reach and range of motion.

❶ Barbell Deadlift, page 32

❷ Dumbbell Pullover, page 46

❸ Barbell Power Clean and Jerk,
page 38

❹ Dips, page 48

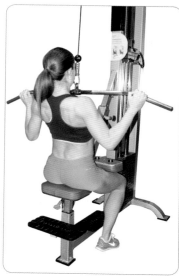

❺ Lat Pulldowns, page 54

6 External Rotation with Band, page 82

7 Hip Extension with Band, page 84

8 Swiss-Ball Jackknife, page 128

9 Stability Ball Exchange, page 132

10 Kneeling Cable Crunch, page 142

MELTING-POT WORKOUT

This workout incorporates many of the different pieces of equipment encountered in the book.

① Barbell Power Clean and Jerk, page 38

② Dumbbell Pullover, page 46

③ Dips, page 48

④ Alternating Kettlebell Row, page 62

⑤ Advanced Kettlebell Windmill, page 72

6 Hip Extension with Band, page 84

7 Box Jumps, page 94

8 Turkish Get-Up, page 112

9 Medicine Ball Pike-Up, page 118

10 Stability Ball Exchange, page 132

KAMIKAZE WORKOUT

This is for the insatiable diehard who wishes to maximise strength, conditioning, stabilisation, agility and athleticism.

❶ Barbell Power Clean and Jerk, page 38

❷ Dips, page 48

❸ Reverse Close-Grip Front Chin, page 52

❹ Alternating Renegade Row, page 64

❺ Plyo Kettlebell Push-Up, page 70

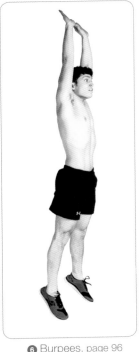

6 Burpees, page 96

7 Mountain Climbers, page 104

8 Star Jumps, page 106

9 Skier, page 110

10 Medicine Ball Pike-Up, page 118

GLOSSARY

GENERAL TERMS

abduction: Movement away from the body.

adduction: Movement towards the body.

anterior: Located in the front.

cardiovascular exercise: Any exercise that increases the heart rate, making oxygen and nutrient-rich blood available to working muscles.

cardiovascular system: The circulatory system that distributes blood throughout the body; it includes the heart, lungs, arteries, veins and capillaries.

core: Refers to the deep muscle layers that lie close to the spine and provide structural support for the entire body. The core is divisible into major core and minor core. The major-core muscles are on the trunk and include the belly area and the mid- and lower back. This area encompasses the pelvic-floor muscles (levator ani, pubococcygeus, iliococcygeus, pubo-rectalis and coccygeus), the abdominals (rectus abdominis, transversus abdominis, obliquus externus and obliquus internus), the spinal extensors (multifidus spinae, erector spinae, splenius, longissimus thoracis and semispinalis) and the diaphragm. The minor core muscles include the latissimus dorsi, gluteus maximus and trapezius (upper, middle and lower). These minor core muscles assist the major muscles when the body engages in activities or movements that require added stability.

crunch: A common abdominal exercise that calls for curling the shoulders towards the pelvis while lying supine with your hands behind the head and your knees bent.

curl: An exercise movement, usually targeting the biceps brachii, that calls for a weight to be moved through an arc, in a 'curling' motion.

deadlift: An exercise movement that calls for lifting a weight, such as a barbell, off the ground from a stabilised bent-over position.

dumbbell: A basic piece of equipment that consists of a short bar on which weight plates are secured. A person can use a dumbbell in one or both hands during an exercise. Most gyms offer dumbbells with the weight plates welded on and the number of kilograms indicated on the plates, but many dumbbells intended for home use come with removable plates that allow you to adjust the weight.

dynamic exercise: An exercise that includes movement through the joints and muscles.

extension: The act of straightening.

extensor muscle: A muscle serving to extend a body part away from the body.

flexion: The bending of a joint.

flexor muscle: A muscle that decreases the angle between two bones, such as bending the arm at the elbow or raising the thigh towards the stomach.

fly: An exercise movement in which the hand and arm move through an arc while the elbow is kept at a constant angle. A fly works the muscles of the upper body.

iliotibial band (ITB): A thick band of fibrous tissue that runs down the outside of the leg, beginning at the hip and extending to the outer side of the tibia, just below the knee joint. The ITB works in conjunction with several of the thigh muscles to provide stability to the outside of the knee joint.

lateral: Located on, or extending towards, the outside.

medial: Located on, or extending towards, the middle.

medicine ball: A small weighted ball that is used in weight training and toning.

neutral position (spine): A spinal position resembling an S shape, consisting of a lordosis (backward curvature) in the lower back, when viewed in profile.

posterior: Located behind.

press: An exercise movement that calls for moving a weight, or other resistance, away from the body.

range of motion: The distance and direction a joint can move between the flexed position and the extended position.

resistance band: Any rubber tubing or flat band device used for strength training that provides a resistive force. Also called a 'fitness band', 'stretching band' and 'stretch tube'.

rotator muscle: One of a group of muscles that assist the rotation of a joint, such as the hip or the shoulder.

scapula: The protrusion of bone on the mid- to upper back. Also known as the 'shoulder blade'.

squat: An exercise that calls for moving the hips back and bending the knees and hips to lower the torso (and an accompanying weight, if desired) and then returning to the upright position. A squat primarily targets the muscles of the thighs, hips and buttocks, as well as the hamstrings.

static exercise: An isometric form of exercise, without movement of the joints, where a position is held for a specific period of time.

Swiss ball: A flexible, inflatable PVC ball, measuring approximately 35 to 86 centimetres in circumference, used for weight training, physical therapy, balance training and other exercise regimens. It is also called a 'balance ball', 'fitness ball', 'stability ball', 'exercise ball', 'gym ball', 'physioball', 'body ball' and many other names.

warm-up: Any form of light exercise of short duration that prepares the body for more intense activity.

weight: Refers to the plates or weight stacks, or the actual poundage listed on the bar or dumbbell.

LATIN TERMS

The following glossary explains the Latin terminology used to describe the body's musculature. Where words are derived from the Greek, this is indicated.

CHEST

coracobrachialis: Greek korakoeidés, 'ravenlike', and brachium, 'arm'

pectoralis (major and minor): pectus, 'breast'

ABDOMEN

obliquus externus: obliquus, 'slanting', and externus, 'outwards'

obliquus internus: obliquus, 'slanting', and internus, 'within'

rectus abdominis: rego, 'straight, upright', and abdomen, 'belly'

serratus anterior: serra, 'saw', and ante, 'before'

transversus abdominis: transversus, 'athwart, across', and abdomen, 'belly'

NECK

scalenus: Greek skalénós, 'unequal'

semispinalis: semi, 'half', and spinae, 'spine'

splenius: Greek spléníon, 'plaster, patch'

sternocleidomastoideus: Greek stérnon, 'chest', Greek kleis, 'key', and Greek mastoeidés, 'breastlike'

BACK

erector spinae: erectus, 'straight', and spinae, 'spine'

latissimus dorsi: latus, 'wide', and dorsum, 'back'

multifidus spinae: multifid, 'to cut into divisions', and spinae, 'spine'

quadratus lumborum: quadratus, 'square, rectangular', and lumbus, 'loin'

rhomboideus: Greek rhembesthai, 'to spin'

trapezius: Greek trapezion, 'small table'

SHOULDERS

deltoideus anterior: Greek deltoeidés, 'delta-shaped' (that is, triangular), and ante, 'before'

deltoideus medialis: Greek deltoeidés, 'delta-shaped' (that is, triangular), and medialis, 'middle'

deltoideus posterior: Greek deltoeidés, 'delta-shaped' (that is, triangular), and posterus, 'behind'

infraspinatus: infra, 'under', and spinae, 'spine'

levator scapulae: levare, 'to raise', and scapulae, 'shoulder [blades]'

subscapularis: sub, 'below', and scapulae, 'shoulder [blades]'

supraspinatus: supra, 'above', and spinae, 'spine'

teres (major and minor): teres, 'rounded'

UPPER ARM

biceps brachii: biceps, 'two-headed', and brachium, 'arm'

brachialis: brachium, 'arm'

triceps brachii: triceps, 'three-headed', and brachium, 'arm'

LOWER ARM

anconeus: Greek anconad, 'elbow'

brachioradialis: brachium, 'arm', and radius, 'spoke'

extensor carpi radialis: extendere, 'to extend', Greek karpós, 'wrist', and radius, 'spoke'

extensor digitorum: extendere, 'to extend', and digitus, 'finger, toe'

flexor carpi pollicis longus: flectere, 'to bend', Greek karpós, 'wrist', pollicis, 'thumb', and longus, 'long'

flexor carpi radialis: flectere, 'to bend', Greek karpós, 'wrist', and radius, 'spoke'

flexor carpi ulnaris: flectere, 'to bend', Greek karpós, 'wrist', and ulnaris, 'forearm'

flexor digitorum: flectere, 'to bend', and digitus, 'finger, toe'

palmaris longus: palmaris, 'palm', and longus, 'long'

pronator teres: pronate, 'to rotate', and teres, 'rounded'

HIPS

gemellus (inferior and superior): geminus, 'twin'

gluteus maximus: Greek gloutós, 'rump', and maximus, 'largest'

gluteus medius: Greek gloutós, 'rump', and medialis, 'middle'

gluteus minimus: Greek gloutós, 'rump', and minimus, 'smallest'

iliacus: ilium, 'groin'

iliopsoas: ilium, 'groin', and Greek psoa, 'groin muscle'

obturator externus: obturare, 'to block', and externus, 'outwards'

obturator internus: obturare, 'to block', and internus, 'within'

pectineus: pectin, 'comb'

piriformis: pirum, 'pear', and forma, 'shape'

quadratus femoris: quadratus, 'square, rectangular', and femur, 'thigh'

UPPER LEG

adductor longus: adducere, 'to contract', and longus, 'long'

adductor magnus: adducere, 'to contract', and magnus, 'major'

biceps femoris: biceps, 'two-headed', and femur, 'thigh'

gracilis: gracilis, 'slim, slender'

rectus femoris: rego, 'straight, upright', and femur, 'thigh'

sartorius: sarcio, 'to patch, to repair'

semimembranosus: semi, 'half', and membrum, 'limb'

semitendinosus: semi, 'half', and tendo, 'tendon'

tensor fasciae latae: tendere, 'to stretch', fasciae, 'band', and latae, 'laid down'

vastus intermedius: vastus, 'immense, huge', and intermedius, 'between'

vastus lateralis: vastus, 'immense, huge', and lateralis, 'side'

vastus medialis: vastus, 'immense, huge', and medialis, 'middle'

LOWER LEG

adductor digiti minimi: adducere, 'to contract', digitus, 'finger, toe', and minimum 'smallest'

adductor hallucis: adducere, 'to contract', and hallex, 'big toe'

extensor digitorum: extendere, 'to extend', and digitus, 'finger, toe'

extensor hallucis: extendere, 'to extend', and hallex, 'big toe'

flexor digitorum: flectere, 'to bend', and digitus, 'finger, toe'

flexor hallucis: flectere, 'to bend', and hallex, 'big toe'

gastrocnemius: Greek gastroknémía, 'calf [of the leg]'

peroneus: peronei, 'of the fibula'

plantaris: planta, 'sole'

soleus: solea, 'sandal'

tibialis anterior: tibia, 'reed pipe', and ante, 'before'

tibialis posterior: tibia, 'reed pipe', and posterus, 'behind'

trochlea tali: trochleae, 'pulley-shaped structure', and talus, 'lower portion of ankle joint'

CREDITS & ACKNOWLEDGEMENTS

PHOTOGRAPHY
Photography by FineArtsPhotoGroup.com
Models: Miguel Carrera, Tara DiLuca
Trainer: Hank Dean

ILLUSTRATIONS
All large illustrations by Hector Aiza/3D Labz Animation India, except
the insets throughout and the full-body anatomy art works on pages
12 and 13: by Linda Bucklin/Shutterstock.

ACKNOWLEDGEMENTS
The author and publisher also offer thanks to those closely involved in
the creation of this book: Moseley Road president Sean Moore, general
manager Karen Prince, art director Tina Vaughan, editorial director
Damien Moore, designer and production director Adam Moore; and
Sands Publishing Solutions editors David and Sylvia Tombesi-Walton
and designer Simon Murrell.

ABOUT THE AUTHOR
Hollis Lance Liebman has been a fitness
magazine editor, national bodybuilding
champion and author. He is a published
physique photographer and has served
as a bodybuilding and fitness-
competition judge. Currently a Los
Angeles resident, Hollis has worked with
some of Hollywood's elite, earning rave
reviews. Visit his website, www.
holliswashere.com, for fitness tips and
complete training programmes. This is
his fourth book.

Author photograph by Sonia Keshishian

AUTHOR'S ACKNOWLEDGEMENTS
This book is dedicated to my two best men: my brother, Marshal W.
Liebman, for his opinions and honesty, lending his ear and proving just
how strong family ties truly are; and my best friend, James J. Kemp Jr,
for his strength, courage, friendship, love and support.

This book belongs to

....

Published in 2021 by Alligator Products Ltd
Cupcake is an imprint of Alligator Products Ltd,
2nd Floor, 314 Regents Park Road, London, N3 2JX
www.alligatorbooks.co.uk

Copyright © 2021 Alligator Products Ltd
Written by Christine Swift
Illustrated by Claire Stimpson

Printed in China.1845

The Penguin King

Written by Christine Swift
Illustrated by Claire Stimpson

cupcake

Peter penguin was little,
there was no doubt about it.

Where Peter lived, there were lots of penguins. They were so tall and regal. Peter dreamed of being like them.

When Peter asked if they wanted to play, they didn't hear him above their noisy regal voices.

When the regal penguins arrived,
everyone listened to them.

Peter felt sad.

When Peter went surfing,
he had the smallest board.

When Peter went fishing,
he had the smallest fishing rod.

"We are all different," said his dad,
"you are great just the way you are".

"Look at the other penguins, I am sure that some of them would like to be just like you"

That's true, thought Peter.   His dad was great!

He was good at ice-sliding.

He was great at swimming.

He was kind to his family.

Peter went for a swim to think about things.

Well, he was bigger than the fish!

Peter found an old fisherman's glove in the water.

He had an idea.

"Penguins, listen to me!" shouted Peter.
EVERYONE looked at him.

"Today, I am KING Peter, and I don't mind having the smallest board or the smallest fishing rod, because I am great, just like my dad!"

"I'm so proud of you, Peter" said his dad. "You are growing into a very fine penguin indeed."

Peter didn't need his king's crown to be heard any more.

The other penguins all listened to Peter,
and were very happy to play with him.